Sharpen Up!

on Michigan Science

BOOK 8

Buckle Dol
PUBLISHING COMP

D1377174

Acknowledgments

The science editors gratefully acknowledge the author team of James A. Shymansky, Larry D. Yore, Michael P. Clough, John A. Craven III, Sandra K. Enger, Laura Henriques, Tracy M. Hogan, Leigh Monhardt, Rebecca M. Monhardt, Jo Anne Ollerenshaw, Lionel Sandner, John W. Tillotson, and Peter Veronesi.

People in Science profiles written by Martha V. Lutz and Richard J. Lutz.

ISBN 0-7836-2348-8

Catalog #SU MI8S 1

2 3 4 5 6 7 8 9 10

President and Publisher: Douglas J. Paul, Ph.D.; Editorial Director: John Hansen; Project Editor: Daniel J. Smith; Editors: Molly Hansen, Paul Meyers; Production Editor: Michael Hankes; Production Director: Jennifer Booth; Production Supervisor: Ginny York; Art Director: Chris Wolf; Graphic Designers: Mary Jo Heil, Diane Hudachek.

Copyright © 2001 by Buckle Down Publishing Company. All rights reserved. No part of this work may be reproduced or transmitted in any form or by any means, electronic or mechanical, including photocopying, recording, or any information storage or retrieval systems, except as may be expressly permitted in writing by the publisher, Buckle Down Publishing Company, P.O. Box 2180, Iowa City, IA 52244-2180.

Cover: Images © 1996 PhotoDisc, Inc.

TABLE OF CONTENTS

© 2001 Buckle Down Publishing Company. DO NOT DUPLICATE.

© 2001 Buckle Down Publishing Company. DO NOT DUPLICATE.

introduction

What do you think of when somebody mentions the word *scientist*? People often picture a very bright person who knows millions of facts about different things and performs elaborate experiments in a lab coat. This isn't quite true. Yes, many scientists are extremely knowledgeable, but not all of them are! Good scientists realize that there is more to science than knowing and remembering something about everything.

One thing that all good scientists have in common is a strong curiosity about what they *don't* know. This curiosity helps them identify gaps in human knowledge—areas where our knowledge is incomplete or where we haven't begun to explore. Only then can they ask useful questions about things that we don't know, and then develop ways to answer those questions and solve the problems they present. The job of scientists is to put their curiosity to work, to make sense of the natural world, and to find explanations for why things happen.

You might not realize it, but you already do many things scientifically. Scientists try to find patterns in the way natural events occur. They make observations and take measurements. They classify things by their qualities. When you check the clouds in the sky to see whether it looks like rain, you are using your knowledge of weather patterns and cloud types. When you try to find a quicker route to school, you are testing a hypothesis and using measurement skills. When you're deciding what breed of dog you want, you are using a system of animal classification. When you try a new skateboard trick, you are applying your knowledge of force and motion. You get the idea.

© 2001 Buckle Down Publishing Company. DO NOT DUPLICATE.

Not everyone is suited for a career in science, and maybe you'll end up in a different career. No matter what you end up doing, science and technology will affect your daily life in the workplace and at home. Twenty years ago, who could have predicted how the Internet, computers, and medical research would have changed life by now? The more you can learn now about how society, science, and technology interact, the better you will adapt to whatever innovations or discoveries may occur. Who knows, maybe you'll be the one who makes the breakthrough!

About This Book

Sharpen up on Michigan Science, Book 8, will help you improve your scientific thinking skills. It will help you to practice and review scientific ways of making decisions and solving real-world problems. You will explore the ways in which scientists arrive at new scientific knowledge. These methods include constructing new knowledge through research and reading, asking good questions, conducting clear experiments, recording data, and sharing and discussing results. You will learn how science works with technology and society to solve problems, and you will analyze some of the negative impacts that these forces have had on the natural world. You will then apply these ideas in reviews of life science, physical science, and Earth and space science.

Sometime this year, you will be asked to demonstrate your understanding of science by taking a state science test. This book will help you review what you need to know to do your best on that test.

About the Test

The written portion of the eighth-grade test will have two kinds of questions: multiple choice and short answer. The multiple-choice questions will ask you to choose one of four answer choices. The short-answer questions will ask you to solve a problem or support a decision by writing your answers. Many of the questions will ask about a picture, graph, diagram, or experiment.

This book will give you plenty of practice answering the types of questions you'll see on the state test. If you work through all the reviews and questions in this book, you will be ready.

Test-Taking Tips

The best way to prepare for any test is to study and review. These test-taking tips will help you make the most of what you know.

For starters, here are several tips to help you tackle the multiple-choice questions on the state test.

Tip 1: Read each question carefully.

You can't answer a question correctly if you don't know what you're being asked. Read each question carefully. Make sure you understand it before going on to the answer choices.

© 2001 Buckle Down Publishing Company. DO NOT DUPLICATE.

Tip 2: Take a close look at any visual information that appears with the question.

Some questions will ask you about a picture, graph, or table. Don't try to answer the question until you've taken a good look at the visual information.

Tip 3: Read each choice carefully.

Make sure the choice you select is the best answer to the question being asked. To do this, you'll need to look at all the choices. Don't pick the first choice that looks good. There may be a better choice down the line.

Tip 4: Answer every question, even if you have to guess.

If you aren't sure of an answer, go ahead and guess. You've got nothing to lose. If you don't answer a question, you can't possibly get it right. If you guess, there's a one-in-four chance that you just might choose the correct answer.

Tip 5: Use your understanding of science to *ZAP*® wrong choices.

Each question will have only one right answer. By getting rid of wrong answers, you increase your chance of choosing the right one. So instead of blind guessing, you need to learn to "Zero-in-And-Pick" — *ZAP* — before you guess. Take a look at the following question.

1. Jill is classifying sea animals into two groups: vertebrates and invertebrates. Which of the following sea animals should go in the vertebrate group?
    A. manta
    B. cuttlefish
    C. crayfish
    D. sponge

You might look at the first three choices and not know whether these sea animals have backbones or not. But look at choice D, sponge. You know a sponge doesn't have a spine. So get rid of D. You now have a one-in-three chance of guessing the correct answer. If you remember that a crayfish looks like a little lobster, you might figure out that C is not a very good answer either. That leaves you with two choices. You now have a 50/50 chance of getting the correct answer (which is A).

Tip 6: Don't let difficult questions slow you down.

If you come to a difficult question, try to *ZAP* the wrong choices. Then make your best guess and move on. Don't let a difficult question make you nervous. The next question might be easier. If you want, you can mark an X next to questions you find hard and come back to them later. Sometimes the correct answer will come to you after you've looked at other questions.

© 2001 Buckle Down Publishing Company. DO NOT DUPLICATE.

Tip 7: Check your work.

If you finish the test early, don't close your test booklet and stare out the window or take a nap. Go back and check your work.

Here are a few tips for answering the short-answer questions on the test. These are the questions for which you have to write an answer in your own words.

Tip 8: Use your best handwriting.

You won't get any extra points for nice handwriting. But if a scorer can't read your answer, you might get zero points!

Tip 9: Answer every short-answer question.

If a short-answer question seems too difficult for you and you're not sure how to answer it, write something anyway. You may know more about the topic than you think.

Tip 10: Look closely at what you're told or shown on the page.

Short-answer questions usually ask you about an experiment or problem or picture of some sort. Often, you will be able to find the answers in the picture, table, graph, or passage that appears with the question. You will likely need to call on your own science knowledge, too. But start with what's right in front of you when you're looking for an answer.

Tip 11: Relax.

If you've studied all the material in this book, you should be ready on test day. If you feel yourself getting a little nervous or stuck, give yourself a quick break. Relax—but not for too long. Take a deep breath. Look for an easy question to get you back into things. Then keep going until you are done. You can do it.

© 2001 Buckle Down Publishing Company. DO NOT DUPLICATE.

unit 1

The Nature of Science

© 2001 Buckle Down Publishing Company. DO NOT DUPLICATE.

Review 1
Scientific Investigations

Decisions, decisions! Bill loves his racing bike for its speed and the way it turns tight corners, but the lightweight wheel spokes often break, resulting in lengthy repairs. He would like to use heavier, more durable spokes, but he's not sure whether these will affect the bike's road performance and speed. He will need to do a **systematic investigation** before he can draw any **conclusions**. This approach is the basis of all good scientific research, and it will help you make decisions in everyday life, as well. Let's take a closer look at how conclusions are drawn in science.

What Do You Think?

Imagine that you have found four bikes that you like, and you need to find out which one is the best racing bike. You can probably think of several measurements that would be useful in identifying the best racing bike.

What would you have to do to make sure you identified the lightest bike?

_____

_____

Finding out which racing bike is the fastest might require a little more thinking.

How would you go about finding the fastest bike?

_____

_____

What People Think

Sound scientific conclusions are based on trustworthy data from systematic investigations. In a systematic investigation, the researcher makes an effort to identify all the things that are involved in the investigation (called **variables**) and to keep track of everything that is done. In this way, cause and effect can be identified, and the experiment can be repeated. In the previous example, it is more difficult to find the fastest bike than it is to find the lightest bike because there are more variables involved: the rider, the road surface, the wind, and so on. In conducting investigations, scientists come up with a statement or a question that can be tested, called a **hypothesis**.

Key Words

conclusion

dependent variable

fair test

hypothesis

independent variable

systematic investigation

variable

© 2001 Buckle Down Publishing Company. DO NOT DUPLICATE.

Then, they usually try to isolate and study one thing (called an **independent variable**) to see how it affects something else (called a **dependent variable**).

In the opening example, Bill wants to replace his current bike spokes with heavier, more durable ones, but he is worried that the new spokes will affect the bike's road performance and speed. If he does a systematic investigation to address this concern, what will be his . . .

independent variable? _____

dependent variable? _____

Most investigations involve other variables that can affect how a dependent variable changes. To get a **fair test** of one independent variable, the other variables have to be kept the same (held constant).

What other variables in Bill's systematic investigation should he try to control?

_____

_____

_____

Even after scientists have done everything systematically, what must they still do to have greater confidence in their conclusion? Explain your answer.

_____

_____

_____

Safety in Investigations

Anytime you begin an investigation, you must first identify any safety issues that might come up. Sometimes this is as simple as setting up a clear workspace with plenty of room and good lighting. Usually, however, you'll need to research the safety precautions first. Whenever you're assembling, repairing, or analyzing a machine, toy, or an appliance, make sure that it is **completely disconnected from any electrical source**, whether that's a wall outlet or a battery. Always read the manual that accompanies the item you're working on because it can identify safety issues that you might not be familiar with. It's also a good idea to ask a teacher or parent for guidance, especially when you're dealing with something new.

© 2001 Buckle Down Publishing Company. DO NOT DUPLICATE.

Using What You Know

Even the most skilled and experienced scientists need to research an idea before they begin an experiment. They read their colleagues' papers on the subject, they explore the library, and they work on the Internet to exchange ideas. Imagine that you notice your bicycle isn't shifting gears very well, so you decide to research the problem. After talking with a friend who knows a little about bicycles, you want to learn how bicycle derailleurs work so that you can adjust yours to make the gears shift more smoothly. You probably need to do some research on derailleur systems before you can successfully solve your gear-shifting problem.

With a partner, find one source on the Internet and one from the library that would help your research on bicycle repair. List them below.

_____

_____

Compare your sources with the derailleur diagram given below. Different terms might be used, but you should be able to use the diagrams to study the derailleur system.

Using the information you have found, describe the basic function of bicycle derailleurs.

_____

_____

_____

_____

_____

_____

_____

_____

_____

_____

_____

_____

**Rear Derailleur
Engaged in High Gear**

low gear
adjustment screw

high gear
adjustment screw

© 2001 Buckle Down Publishing Company. DO NOT DUPLICATE.

Think It Over

Directions: Using the information you have collected from your sources, answer the following questions with your partner. (You may have to go back and do more research.)

1. What may cause a derailleur to need adjusting?

_____

_____

_____

_____

2. List some possible derailleur adjustments that could improve your shifting.

_____

_____

_____

_____

3. How could you systematically investigate which adjustments your bicycle may need to make its gears shift more smoothly?

_____

_____

_____

© 2001 Buckle Down Publishing Company. DO NOT DUPLICATE.

Practice Questions

1. Three eighth graders want to find out what ramp height causes a marble to roll the farthest. How should they set up the investigation?

    A. Set up the same ramp at different heights and use one marble.

    B. Set up three different ramps at different heights and use one marble.

    C. Set up the same ramp at the same height and use three different marbles.

    D. Set up three different ramps at the same height and use three different marbles.

2. To conduct the systematic marble-and-ramp investigation described in Number 1, which of the following would provide the most useful data?

    A. camera

    B. balance

    C. stopwatch

    D. meterstick

3. The students decide to create a graph to illustrate the data collected. How should the x-axis and y-axis be labeled?

    A. x-axis: height of ramp
       y-axis: speed of marble

    B. x-axis: speed of marble
       y-axis: distance marble travels

    C. x-axis: speed of marble
       y-axis: height of ramp

    D. x-axis: height of ramp
       y-axis: distance marble travels

4. Why is it a good idea to take an average of several measurements rather than take just one measurement?

    A. The average accounts for other variables that might affect the measurement.

    B. If you get different measurements, it means that you can't use any of the data.

    C. Taking several measurements means that the investigation is more systematic.

    D. If you make a graph, it is easier to use just one number rather than several numbers.

© 2001 Buckle Down Publishing Company. DO NOT DUPLICATE.

5. Isaac is trying to decide which of two skateboards to buy. He wants the one that will give the longer ride off a ramp. Which of the following procedures would give the best data to help him make his decision?

A. Weigh each of the skateboards to see which is heavier.

B. Measure the length of each skateboard to see which is longer.

C. Ride each skateboard down a ramp to see which one takes him farther.

D. Give the wheels on each skateboard a spin and see which wheels spin longer.

PEOPLE IN SCIENCE

Benjamin Banneker
(United States 1731–1806)

Benjamin Banneker's neighbors wondered about him. Instead of working on his family farm during the day, he wandered around the neighborhood at night, wearing a cloak. What probably looked like some kind of craziness, however, actually was serious work. Banneker, a free-born African American from Maryland, was recording the movement of stars, tides, and the Moon. In 1791, he produced a handwritten almanac. In 1792, he found a publisher, and for 10 years Banneker updated his almanac every year. People said it was the most complete book of its kind. The book had a calendar and showed phases of the Moon, times of high and low tides, the best times to plant, and other useful information. Banneker also included stories and riddles to make his readers laugh and to teach them things. One of his readers was a man who thought of the almanac as proof that all men truly were created equal. That man was Thomas Jefferson, one of Banneker's many admirers. Banneker also served as an assistant to Pierre Charles L'Enfant, a French engineer who designed the plan for Washington, D.C. Before the completion of the project, however, L'Enfant became angry with the project's progress and returned to France, taking the drawings with him. Banneker redrew the plans from memory, allowing Washington, D.C., to be built on schedule.

© 2001 Buckle Down Publishing Company. DO NOT DUPLICATE.

Review 2
Scientific Inquiry

It's going to be another dreary Monday at school, Susan thought as she walked into the classroom. But the gloom turned to noise and excitement when Sean cried, "Come see the baby guppies! There must be 50 of them, and they all look different!" Ben chimed in, saying, "And four of our snails croaked! It must be because the guppies were born."

Ben's idea about why the snails died is called an **inference**, or an idea based on limited factual information. We make inferences like Ben's every day. Scientists must make inferences, too. Read on to find out more about scientific inquiry, including processes such as observation, measurement, and inference.

What Do You Think?

As you will see in Review 2, scientists use systematic investigations to test their initial ideas, often referred to as **hypotheses**, and to gather vital information, called **data**.

What evidence does Ben have for thinking the guppies caused the four snails to die?

_____

_____

_____

What do you think about the accuracy of Ben's inference?

_____

_____

_____

Write one question based on the observations of Ben, Susan, and Sean that addresses the relationship between the guppies and the snails.

_____

_____

_____

Key Words

conclusion

data

global warming

greenhouse effect

hypothesis

inference

model

system

© 2001 Buckle Down Publishing Company. DO NOT DUPLICATE.

What People Think

Scientists would say that although the death of four snails occurred in the same time period as the birth of the guppies, that doesn't mean there is any link between the two events. You may have heard the statement "Association is not causation." In other words, just because two or more events happen together, that doesn't mean one event *causes* the other.

For example, you know from experience that daylight follows the darkness of night, yet the darkness does not cause the daylight. The darkness and the following daylight are *strongly associated*, which means that one always accompanies the other. However, you know that the cause for daylight is not actually the darkness, but rather the rotation of the Earth in relation to the Sun.

Think of another example where an event is always followed by another event but is not caused by that event.

_____

_____

_____

_____

Scientists are currently investigating the rising average world temperature, called **global warming**. This warming trend is associated with increasing atmospheric levels of carbon dioxide. How might carbon dioxide cause this warming? Much of the energy that comes from the Sun is radiated from Earth back out into space. But certain chemicals (such as carbon dioxide) in the atmosphere keep some of this energy from leaving the Earth. These built-up chemicals act like the closed windows of a car, trapping extra heat; this is called the **greenhouse effect**.

Some scientists do not believe that the data support the **conclusion** that human activity is the cause of global warming. They claim the current rise in temperature is merely part of the long-term pattern of changes in the average temperature and is natural in cause. However, many other scientists believe that automobiles, factories, farms, and homes are producing far more carbon, sulfur, and nitrogen gases; they also believe that the more these chemicals are produced and released into the atmosphere, the more likely it is that the overall temperature of the Earth will gradually rise. (You can read more about this problem in Review 15.)

Clouds also can keep heat from escaping the Earth's atmosphere, although they do not contribute to global warming.

© 2001 Buckle Down Publishing Company. DO NOT DUPLICATE.

What happens on cloudy winter nights that illustrates the effects of clouds? How is this different from what happens on clear winter nights?

_____

_____

_____

_____

All greenhouse gases exist in small amounts in our atmosphere. The atmospheric gas most responsible for absorbing radiant energy is carbon dioxide. Venus and Earth are about the same size and are fairly close together. They also both have an atmosphere and clouds. They seem so similar that they frequently have been called the "twin planets." But one important difference is that the atmosphere of Venus is composed of 97% carbon dioxide, whereas less than 1% of Earth's atmosphere is carbon dioxide.

With this information, make inferences about the conditions on Venus, and then compare them with what you know about conditions on Earth.

_____

_____

_____

_____

© 2001 Buckle Down Publishing Company. DO NOT DUPLICATE.

Using What You Know

In this activity, you will design and conduct an investigation to test the hypothesis of the greenhouse effect. Your teacher will provide you with two foam cups filled halfway with soil and a piece of plastic wrap. On the side of each cup, there will be a hole where you will place the end of a thermometer. Both cups will go equal distances from a lamp, which will act as the Sun. This set-up is called the **system**, and it will act as a **model** for the atmospheric system of Earth.

Now you and your partner must create a step-by-step procedure to determine the effect of trapped energy on the system. Your procedure should contain clear instructions and any sketches necessary for another student to follow what you've done without your help. Your results need to be clearly recorded and interpreted using the appropriate method of scientific communications and analysis.

© 2001 Buckle Down Publishing Company. DO NOT DUPLICATE.

Think It Over

1. What was the difference between your experimental and control system?

   _____

   _____

   _____

2. Why is a control system needed in this investigation?

   _____

   _____

   _____

3. Which cup of soil experienced greater temperature change during the experiment? Why?

   _____

   _____

   _____

4. What is the importance of measurement devices, such as a thermometer, in conducting scientific investigations?

   _____

   _____

   _____

© 2001 Buckle Down Publishing Company. DO NOT DUPLICATE.

Practice Questions

1. Which of the following is not a method scientists use to collect evidence?
   A. making direct observations with the five senses
   B. taking direct measurements with tools and other technologies
   C. taking indirect measurements of things that cannot be observed with the five senses
   D. making educated guesses based on past experience and the results of past experiments

2. Which of the following is a likely side effect of an increase in global temperatures?
   A. rise in sea level
   B. formation of large glaciers
   C. increase in volcanic activity
   D. decrease in atmospheric pressure

3. In which of the following places would you most likely experience a natural example of the greenhouse effect?
   A. a desert with hot, dry air and a clear sky
   B. a warm, humid jungle with a cloudy sky
   C. a glacier field, with cold, dry air and a cloudless sky
   D. a seaside town with mild, moist air and a few clouds

4. Which of these actions would most likely limit the greenhouse effect?
   A. limit the amount of land used for forests
   B. release chemicals into the atmosphere
   C. cut pollution emissions from cars and factories
   D. conserve water usage in factories and homes

© 2001 Buckle Down Publishing Company. DO NOT DUPLICATE.

Directions: Use the following graph to answer Numbers 5 and 6.

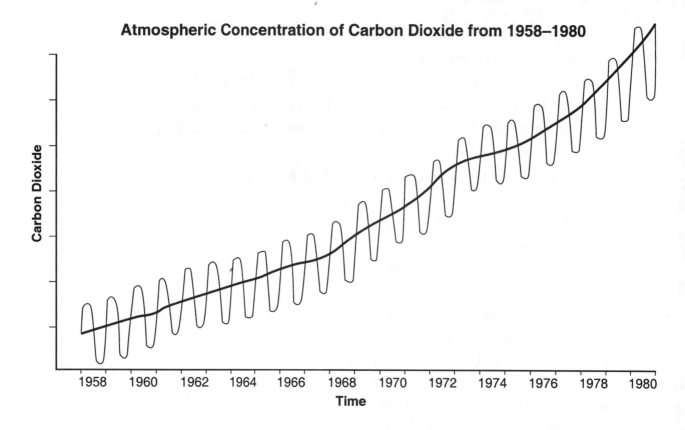

Atmospheric Concentration of Carbon Dioxide from 1958–1980

Carbon Dioxide

1958 1960 1962 1964 1966 1968 1970 1972 1974 1976 1978 1980

Time

5. Which statement best accounts for the pattern of peaks and valleys in the graph?
   A. Human actions create more CO_2 during certain periods of each year.
   B. The sensitivity of the instrument used caused inaccuracies in measurement.
   C. Volcanoes are more active during certain periods of the year, expelling more CO_2 at those times.
   D. CO_2 is removed from the air by plants during the summer and returned in winter as the plants decay.

6. What best accounts for the general trend in the graph?
   A. The energy output of the Sun is increasing.
   B. Volcanoes have recently been more active and are expelling more CO_2.
   C. Human actions are creating less CO_2 than organisms use in photosynthesis.
   D. Human actions are creating more CO_2 than organisms use in photosynthesis.

© 2001 Buckle Down Publishing Company. DO NOT DUPLICATE.

Review 3
Critical Analysis

You're walking into the school building one morning when you meet your best friend. Instead of greeting you as she always does, however, she crosses to the other side of the hallway and doesn't even look at you. There's obviously a problem here. You immediately begin to think about what it could be. *Was it something I said? Was it something I did? Maybe she didn't see me. Maybe she's got something else on her mind today.* You think carefully before deciding what you should do next. You talk to some of your other friends, gathering evidence. You examine the problem from every angle before deciding what to do about it.

Believe it or not, this investigative process is similar to that of scientists. They investigate puzzling problems by thinking carefully about them. They examine evidence. They make decisions based on their investigation and evidence. This process allows them to find explanations for many kinds of problems.

What Do You Think?

Finding problems, asking questions, collecting information, and pursuing explanations are what scientific inquiry is all about. Scientists may state their questions in various ways. Read the following passage and then answer the questions.

Those annoying mosquitoes

Mosquitoes can be a real nuisance because their bite causes discomfort to most people. Only the female mosquito bites. She needs to collect blood from other animals to lay her eggs. The fertilized eggs are laid in a wet area such as a swamp, and mosquito development proceeds through the stages of egg, larva, pupa, and adult. The first three stages occur in water.

Some mosquitoes can be more than just pests, however. Many species of mosquitoes carry diseases that affect people and other animals. We use many different methods to keep mosquitoes of all kinds away from us. For example, many people use lotions or sprays on their skin to repel mosquitoes. We also spray areas with pesticides, burn citronella candles, and use bug zappers to control mosquitoes and keep them from biting.

Sometimes wet, swampy areas are drained in an attempt to control mosquito populations. Explain why this could be effective in controlling mosquitoes. Underline at least one sentence in the paragraphs above that provides information to support your answer.

_____

_____

_____

_____

Key Words

critical thinking

degree of confidence

probability

© 2001 Buckle Down Publishing Company. DO NOT DUPLICATE.

Sometimes a thin layer of oil is sprayed on the surface of the water to control mosquitoes. Why would this approach be effective?

_____

_____

_____

Why is it important to know something about mosquito development and life cycles when trying to find ways to control them?

_____

_____

_____

What People Think

Critical thinking is thinking clearly and logically about a problem or issue, gathering all the evidence available, and making an informed and fair decision about what to believe or do. Critical thinking is useful in every subject area of school and in every part of your life. The choices you make each day require critical thinking: thinking about alternative approaches, clarifying issues, making fair and informed judgments, and being able to give solid reasons for your decisions.

Name a practical problem or decision in your life that required critical thinking, and write about how you went about resolving it.

_____

_____

_____

_____

© 2001 Buckle Down Publishing Company. DO NOT DUPLICATE.

Here's an example of how critical thinking about scientific, technological, and social issues is important.

Nuclear power plants are supposed to generate lots of inexpensive electricity. Many plants are very expensive to operate, however. In addition, nuclear plants create nuclear waste, which is difficult to dispose of because it remains toxic for thousands of years. There is also a risk that radiation might escape if a plant malfunctions. But it would be costly to replace the existing nuclear plants, and the coal-burning plants that might replace them would increase pollution.

Thinking critically about this issue requires weighing all of the alternatives against one another. What should we do about nuclear plants? Which is more important, having nuclear plants as a source of electricity in spite of their problems, or shutting them down and facing problems that may arise when they no longer operate?

Here's another example: Freon is a substance used in appliances such as air conditioners to cool things off. It has been linked to the breakdown of the ozone layer, a serious environmental problem. We want cool homes, cars, and offices in the summertime, but we also want to preserve the planet. Deciding what is right in this case is not an easy decision. It requires critical thinking.

Issues such as nuclear energy and Freon are complex. There are good arguments to be made on either side. It's exactly because of this that people need to consider these issues and use their critical thinking skills to arrive at an informed opinion.

What is another example of a scientific or technological problem that presents difficult questions for society? What are some of the questions that this problem raises?

_____

_____

_____

_____

As the examples above demonstrate, scientists must often interpret information that isn't always crystal clear. There are usually two or more sides to a scientific issue, especially those that involve a social concern, such as energy use. Good scientific thinking requires us to state the **degree of confidence** we have in our findings. If you read a scientific report on an experiment, you won't often find words like *never* or *always*. This isn't because scientists are afraid to make a claim; rather, they know that their findings will be most useful to others if they report all the possible problems with the results. Scientists know that it is just as important to state their degree of confidence in the results as it is to report any exciting new discoveries. A cautious claim is usually seen as the strongest kind.

© 2001 Buckle Down Publishing Company. DO NOT DUPLICATE.

You can apply this critical thinking to your everyday life. Imagine you find a newspaper article entitled "Abominable Snowman Discovered in Alaska." You read the article, which contains many eyewitness reports, some photographs, and precise measurements of footprints.

How would you rate your degree of confidence in the story, on a scale of 1 to 10? Explain why you rated your confidence this way.

_____

_____

As you come to the end of the article, you notice a line that reads "Information for this article was gathered by the Society for the Discovery of the Yeti."

Given this new information, how would you rate your confidence now? Again, explain why you rated your confidence this way.

_____

_____

When you read an article in the newspaper, when a scientist reports her findings, or when a town must choose whether to install a nuclear reactor, the probability of various circumstances must be considered before making a decision.

Probability is the chance that a certain event will or will not occur. Every time you listen to a weather forecast, you know that the meteorologist has weighed the probability of numerous weather events against each other. This is a very important intersection of mathematics and science: Through probability, scientists state with numbers what their degree of confidence is for a particular finding. For example, imagine you're watching a weather forecast in January. The meteorologist mentions a warm front gathering in the Gulf of Mexico and a cold front massing in Canada. The probability that the warm front will push all the way into Michigan during the winter is low, but the probability that the cold front will come south into Michigan is relatively high. Each decision made by the meteorologist is based on probability, the mathematical chance of an event occurring.

Mathematical probability expresses chance as a ratio or percentage. It is determined by calculating the number of desired or undesired events then dividing that number by the number of total possible events.

What is the probability of rolling a 4 on a six-sided die? Explain your answer.

_____

_____

© 2001 Buckle Down Publishing Company. DO NOT DUPLICATE.

Using What You Know

When scientists conduct an experiment, it's important for them to know whether the results are being caused by something specific or whether the results are happening by chance. They use probability to determine whether something other than chance is contributing to the results.

In this activity, you will need two pennies, a cup, and a pencil or pen.

Step 1: If you flip the penny, you have two possible outcomes: heads or tails.

If you flip one penny 50 times, how many times would you expect heads? How many times would you expect tails?

Step 2: Place one penny in the cup. Cover the cup with your hand. Shake the cup and then tip the penny out onto your desk. Write down your results (heads or tails). Do this 50 times. Tally your tosses in the space below.

If you were to toss this penny 1,000 times, how many times would you expect to get heads?

Step 3: If you were to flip two pennies, what are the possible combinations of heads and tails on the coins?

To determine the expected results of tossing two pennies, you will need to do a bit of critical thinking and mathematical reasoning.

To find the number of expected double heads:

What is the chance that the first penny will turn up as a head?

© 2001 Buckle Down Publishing Company. DO NOT DUPLICATE.

What is the chance that the second penny will turn up as a head?

_____

What is the chance that both pennies will turn up as heads?

_____

To find the number of expected double tails:

What is the chance that the first penny will turn up as a tail?

_____

What is the chance that the second penny will turn up as a tail?

_____

What is the chance that both pennies will turn up as tails?

_____

What is the chance that one penny will turn up as heads and the other penny will turn up as tails?

_____

Step 4: Place two pennies in the cup.

Toss the two pennies together 50 times and record your results in the table below.

Combinations	Tally	Total
Heads/heads		
Heads/tails or Tails/heads		
Tails/tails		

© 2001 Buckle Down Publishing Company. DO NOT DUPLICATE.

Think It Over

Directions: Use the information from the previous section to answer the questions in this section.

1. When you tossed just one penny, how did your observed results compare with the expected results?

    _____

    _____

    _____

2. When you tossed two pennies, how did your observed results compare with the expected results?

    _____

    _____

    _____

3. Do you think your penny-tossing results were affected by anything other than chance? Give reasons for your answer.

    _____

    _____

    _____

4. After completing the penny tosses, some people in the class were probably very close to the expected results. Others may have had results that were different from what was expected.

    How would increasing the number of tosses affect how well the observed number of double heads, double tails, or heads/tails combinations match the expected outcomes?

    _____

    _____

    _____

    _____

© 2001 Buckle Down Publishing Company. DO NOT DUPLICATE.

Practice Questions

1. If you flip a dime 200 times, what is the expected number of heads?
   A. 50
   B. 100
   C. 125
   D. 150

2. If you toss two quarters at the same time for 400 tosses, how many times would you predict that you would get the combination of one head and one tail?
   A. 50 times
   B. 75 times
   C. 100 times
   D. 200 times

3. People who live near Acme Chemical Company were surveyed about the health of the trees, plants, and grass in their yards. When the survey results were reported, it was noted that 32% of the oak trees growing close to the company's plant had died or were showing signs of disease, which was more than twice the national average.

   Who would most likely have the highest level of concern about this potential problem?
   A. People who use plant fertilizer on their trees.
   B. People who have yards with maple trees.
   C. People who have yards with oak trees and live close to the plant.
   D. People in a neighboring city who have oak trees in their yards.

4. There is an old saying about mosquitoes: "For each mosquito controlled in May, you will save 1,000 mosquito bites in August." What information do you need to critically analyze the accuracy of this statement? Explain how you would use this information and your critical thinking to evaluate the statement.

   _____

   _____

   _____

   _____

© 2001 Buckle Down Publishing Company. DO NOT DUPLICATE.

Review 4
Science, Technology, and Human Affairs

Technology affects you in hundreds of ways. Citizens of developed countries depend on technology 24 hours a day to make life easier, safer, and more enjoyable. But technology also has negative effects. You have probably seen one of the many science fiction movies that show a computer or a robot "going bad" and turning against humans. The real negative effects of technology aren't quite so exciting, but these movies do demonstrate some of the tensions between **science**, **technology**, and **society**. This review focuses on the ways in which these three forces affect one another, positively and negatively.

What Do You Think?

Technology is part of almost every aspect of our lives, from transportation to communication to night baseball games.

The following chart lists six examples of common technologies in our lives. Describe one positive and one negative effect of each example. The first one has been filled in for you.

Technology	Positive Effects	Negative Effects
Personal stereos	allows you to listen to music wherever you go	decreases conversation between people
Nuclear power		
Cellular telephones		
Organ transplants		
Automobiles		
Plastics		

Key Words

design	science	system
model	society	technology

© 2001 Buckle Down Publishing Company. DO NOT DUPLICATE.

What People Think

People often confuse science with technology. Although science and technology overlap a great deal, they are different. Scientists use inquiry to produce knowledge about the natural world. Technologists use **design** to create products and processes that address people's needs. It is often impossible to predict how a particular breakthrough in scientific knowledge might be applied as technology. For example, when Ben Franklin discovered the connection between lightning and electricity, he had no idea that his discovery would eventually lead to such things as hand-held computers. Technologists not only create useful products for society, they also invent instruments necessary for scientists to understand nature better. In this way, modern science and technology depend upon each other.

> List at least three different technologies you have used in science experiments, and explain how each helped you in the experiment.

_____

_____

_____

_____

_____

In addition, society influences science and technology. Both state and federal governments, which represent society, provide money for scientific research and technological developments. Each year, billions of state and federal tax dollars are spent on numerous scientific projects. Some examples of these government-funded research projects include finding cures for diseases; making discoveries about everything from subatomic particles to the origins of the universe; and inventing, designing, and producing devices that increase food production, conserve energy, clean up polluted lakes, and solve other technological problems facing people. Not all these research projects make everyone happy. A quick look at the daily news reports on TV will show people protesting a scientific or technological issue, such as a nuclear plant, global warming, world population growth, or genetically engineered plants and foods.

© 2001 Buckle Down Publishing Company. DO NOT DUPLICATE.

Check your local newspaper to locate an article about how society is affecting science or technology. Summarize the critical theme of the article.

_____

_____

_____

_____

_____

_____

Common themes connect ideas within and between science and technology. Two tools that occur frequently in science and technology are the use of **systems** and **models**. Scientists, engineers, and students find these big ideas useful when thinking about computers, planets, stars, automobiles, human bodies, volcanoes, and other things.

Use your memory, science books, a dictionary, and other references to understand what these big ideas are all about. Write down a brief explanation of each.

Systems and subsystems:_____

_____

_____

Models: _____

_____

_____

© 2001 Buckle Down Publishing Company. DO NOT DUPLICATE.

You know that scientific knowledge affects technology, and technological advances can push scientific knowledge far beyond its former boundaries. But scientific knowledge can also directly affect society. For instance, when scientists showed that certain creatures may be more intelligent than we previously thought, it helped to spur the recent animal-rights movement. In return, society affects both science and technology. For example, people worldwide are concerned about energy supplies. We want to be sure that we have a long-lasting supply of materials to create energy without polluting the environment. For this reason, much money is directed toward areas of science and technology that explore cleaner, renewable fuels.

How does society affect medical research?

_____

_____

_____

_____

_____

_____

_____

All technology has hidden benefits and costs, and these change society in positive and negative ways. Citizens, including yourself, must become aware of the choices society makes when particular technologies are adopted. To make intelligent choices, you must learn to stand back and ask questions about technology.

© 2001 Buckle Down Publishing Company. DO NOT DUPLICATE.

Using What You Know

Television changed society drastically when it first became available to the general public in the late 1940s. Imagine your life without TV! It might not be as bad as you think. Team up with one or two classmates and make a list of the ways in which your life, your family's life, and society as a whole would be different if there were no television to watch. Use the spaces that follow for your list, and try to think of more than one response for each question.

Where would you get daily news? _____

_____

What would you do for entertainment? _____

_____

How would you learn about new ideas? _____

_____

Whose jobs would be most affected? _____

_____

How would school be different? _____

_____

List as many other things as you can that would be different: _____

_____

_____

_____

_____

_____

_____

© 2001 Buckle Down Publishing Company. DO NOT DUPLICATE.

Think It Over

1. What technology, other than television, would you miss the most if it disappeared? Why?

_____

_____

_____

_____

2. What technology do you think has had the greatest positive impact on today's society? Why?

_____

_____

_____

_____

3. What technology do you think has had the greatest negative impact on today's society? Why?

_____

_____

_____

_____

© 2001 Buckle Down Publishing Company. DO NOT DUPLICATE.

Practice Questions

1. Which statement most accurately describes the effects of technology on society?
   A. Its effects are invisibly positive.
   B. Its effects are visibly negative.
   C. Its effects are visibly positive and negative.
   D. Its effects are visibly and invisibly positive and negative.

2. Which piece of scientific equipment is the most recent technological development?

   A.

   C.

   B.

   D.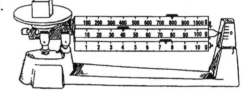

3. Which of the following is the most accurate statement?
   A. New technology costs more than old technology.
   B. New technology is always based on scientific theories or methods.
   C. New technology changes the way humans work, think, and interact.
   D. New technology always ends up replacing old technology because it is better.

4. Which of the following is not a case of technological advancement?
   A. the theory of relativity
   B. the invention of the microscope
   C. the discovery and control of fire
   D. the development of a polio vaccine

© 2001 Buckle Down Publishing Company. DO NOT DUPLICATE.

5. Use arrows to show how science, technology, and society interact and affect each other.

Science   Technology

Society

Write a short paragraph explaining and giving reasons for your arrows.

_____

_____

_____

_____

_____

_____

_____

_____

PEOPLE IN SCIENCE

Lloyd A. Hall
(United States 1894–1971)

Have you ever wondered how foods like Twinkies can stay fresh seemingly forever? It's because they're filled with *preservatives*. We can thank Lloyd A. Hall for the preservative industry that allows meats, breads, cereals, spices, and even medicines to stay fresh for long periods of time. Before Hall did his work, people had trouble keeping foods fresh. When preservatives were added, they often ruined the taste of food. Then along came Hall, who was a food chemist working with sodium nitrates and nitrites. He developed a successful combination of these salts that lets foods stay fresh while keeping their flavor. Hall worked for various food companies during his career. During World War II, he worked for the U.S. government to create foods for soldiers. He developed more than 100 patents in the United States, Britain, and Canada. After his retirement, he worked as a consultant to the Food and Agriculture Organization of the United Nations.

© 2001 Buckle Down Publishing Company. DO NOT DUPLICATE.

unit **2**

Life Science

© 2001 Buckle Down Publishing Company. DO NOT DUPLICATE.

Review 5
Plant and Animal Cells

Do you like to put together jigsaw puzzles? Trying to re-create a picture by putting together hundreds of tiny pieces can be challenging. Individual pieces by themselves don't give much of an idea what the final picture will look like, yet each piece is important in creating the whole.

Cells are like puzzle pieces; they work together to form a structure. Cells are the building blocks of living things. Some organisms are made up of only one cell, which performs all the functions necessary to keep the organism alive. In more complex organisms, specialized cells form **tissues**, tissues form **organs**, and organs form **systems**. This review will give you a more in-depth look at cells, the structure of cells, and what cells do.

What Do You Think?

You already know that all living things are made up of cells. But are all cells alike? Think for a moment about the cells that make up your body.

How are all the cells of your body alike?

_____

_____

_____

_____

How are the cells of your body different?

_____

_____

_____

_____

_____

Key Words

cell

mitochondria

mitosis

multicellular

organ

organelle

system

tissue

unicellular

© 2001 Buckle Down Publishing Company. DO NOT DUPLICATE.

What People Think

Have you ever seen pictures of blood cells? People can get confused and think that living things contain cells rather than understanding that all living things are made up of cells. Our blood does not simply have cells that float around in it. Blood itself is actually made up of cells. It's amazing to think that the human body is made up of about a trillion cells! But when you remember that cells are so tiny that you have to use a microscope to see them, a trillion becomes a bit easier to imagine.

Why do people often refer to cells as "the building blocks of living things"?

_____

_____

_____

Within each cell is a mixture of liquids and tiny structures, called **organelles**, that are constantly moving, growing, changing, and multiplying. Each organelle has a special form and purpose in the operation, maintenance, repair, and reproduction of the cell. The basic parts of a plant cell are shown in the following diagram.

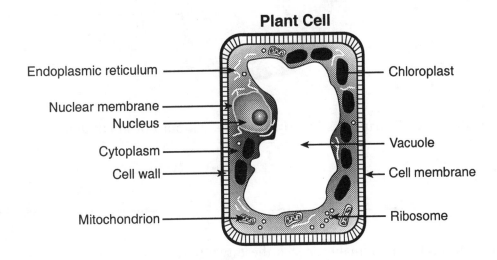

Plant Cell

The following list briefly explains the function of each labeled component.

Cell membrane: semipermeable membrane that controls movement of molecules in and out of the cell

Nucleus: control center for all cell activity; contains chromosomes, which carry the genes that help the organism reproduce

Nuclear membrane: encloses the cell nucleus

Vacuoles: cavities inside the cell cytoplasm that store fluids and dissolved materials

© 2001 Buckle Down Publishing Company. DO NOT DUPLICATE.

Mitochondria: organelles that release energy to support all cell activity

Endoplasmic reticulum: ribbon-like system that transports materials within the cell

Cytoplasm: clear, thick fluid that holds all the components of a cell

Ribosomes: organelles that contain the enzymes which help produce proteins

Chloroplasts: organelles that contain chlorophyll used in photosynthesis

Cell wall: the outer, nonliving cellulose structure that helps the cell keep its shape

Following is a diagram of an animal cell. Label the parts of this cell using the terms in the list for the plant cell. You will notice that two cell structures from the plant cell are not found in the animal cell.

Animal Cell

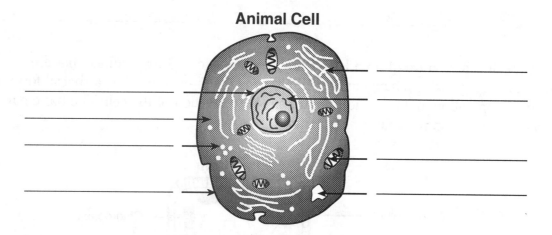

What are the two cell structures found in a plant cell but not in an animal cell?

_____

_____

Why do you think that animal cells lack these two parts?

_____

_____

_____

© 2001 Buckle Down Publishing Company. DO NOT DUPLICATE.

Some organisms, such as the amoeba, are **unicellular**, which means they have just one cell. That cell must carry on all the organism's life functions. Humans, on the other hand, are **multicellular**. Not only are humans made up of trillions of cells, but we also have many different kinds of cells. You can imagine the problems that would occur if each human cell had to do everything involved in being a human. And think what you would look like if all of your trillions of cells were exactly the same!

An important change in the history of cells was the evolution of the **mitochondria**. These organelles are often called the powerhouses of cells because they are responsible for the energy production for each cell. In animal cells, for example, the mitochondria take the food molecules transported by the blood and break them down; this process releases the energy that a cell needs to stay alive and function. This is happening constantly throughout an animal's body. Unicellular organisms that developed mitochondria were able to process food much more efficiently, and this gave rise to multicellular organisms.

Usually, the greater the number of cells an organism has, the greater variety of cells it has. The different kinds of cells are organized into systems that perform different jobs for the body. Think about some of the things that humans need to have and do to stay alive. Each of these functions (breathing, eating, thinking, and so on) is made possible by groups of specialized cells that are arranged into tissues, organs, and systems.

For each of the following types of specialized cells, briefly describe how you think the cell contributes to the overall function of its particular system. The first one has been completed for you.

nerve cell (animal): *carries electrical impulses* _____

muscle cell (animal): _____

red blood cell (animal): _____

root cell (plant): _____

stem cell (plant): _____

leaf cell (plant): _____

© 2001 Buckle Down Publishing Company. DO NOT DUPLICATE.

Using What You Know

Mitosis is the term used to describe the process of one cell dividing into two complete cells. But how does mitosis work? Do the following activity to help you understand. You will need a 24-inch piece of string, scissors, and four colored toothpicks: two of one color and two of another color.

Step 1: Make a circle with the string. Place the four toothpicks in the circle.

Step 2: Remove the circle of string. Using the scissors, cut each toothpick in half. Line up the toothpicks on your desk, each half opposite its old half.

Step 3: Cut your string in half. Make two circles with your string. Place two of the same colored toothpick halves into one circle and their matching colored pair into the other circle. Repeat this with the other colored toothpicks.

Step 4: Repeat Steps 2 and 3 to produce two pairs of identical "cells."

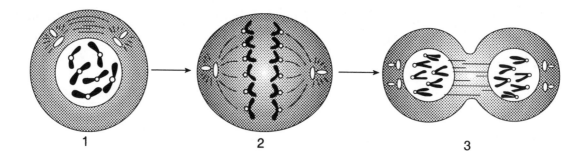

1   2   3

© 2001 Buckle Down Publishing Company. DO NOT DUPLICATE.

Think It Over

1. What part of the cell does the string represent in your model of mitosis?

   _____

   What parts do the toothpicks represent?

   _____

2. Why were two toothpicks of one color and two toothpicks of another used in Step 1?

   _____

   _____

   _____

3. This string-and-toothpick model is different from real cells in many ways, one being the fact that the string and toothpick pieces get smaller and smaller, while dividing cells stay the same size as the original cell. How do the dividing cells maintain their size?

   _____

   _____

   _____

4. How many cells would you have when the four cells undergo mitosis one more time? Three more times? Ten more times?

   _____

   _____

   _____

© 2001 Buckle Down Publishing Company. DO NOT DUPLICATE.

Practice Questions

1. Which of the following correctly identifies the function of the given cell component?
   A. vacuoles: control the activity of the cell
   B. ribosomes: involved with storing and releasing energy
   C. cytoplasm: outer structure that helps the cell keep its shape
   D. cell membrane: controls movement of materials into and out of the cell

2. Which of the following is the control center of both plant and animal cells?
   A. nucleus
   B. ribosomes
   C. protoplasm
   D. endoplasmic reticulum

3. If a cell has a large number of mitochondria, what can you predict about this cell?
   A. The cell is getting ready to subdivide.
   B. The cell will have the same number of nuclei.
   C. The cell requires much energy to function properly.
   D. The cell is old and many of the mitochondria no longer work.

4. Describe how animal and plant cells are alike and how they are different.

   Alike: _____

   _____

   Different: _____

   _____

Directions: Use the following drawings of types of human cells to answer Numbers 5 and 6.

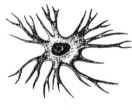

| A | B | C | D |

5. Which of the cells relaxes and contracts?
   A. A   B. B   C. C   D. D

6. Which cell carries impulses?
   A. A   B. B   C. C   D. D

© 2001 Buckle Down Publishing Company. DO NOT DUPLICATE.

Review 6
Classifying Animals

"I hate insects!" Sarah cried as she leaped away from the spider near her desk. "Why can't they stay where they belong?"

Looking bored, Kendra said, "It's a spider, not an insect, and where exactly should it be?"

"Bugs, insects, spiders, crawly things—they're all the same to me," Sarah said.

But are they really all the same? In this review, you will see how scientists classify living things to better understand and learn more about them.

What Do You Think?

Sarah and Kendra were demonstrating their understanding of the classification of living things.

Why is a classification system for living things valuable to people?

_____

_____

_____

_____

Why might Sarah and lots of other people misclassify the spider?

_____

_____

_____

_____

Key Words

arthropod
circulatory system
class
digestive system
endocrine system
excretory system
family
genus
invertebrate
kingdom
nervous system
order
organ system
phylum
respiratory system
skeletal system
species
vertebrate

© 2001 Buckle Down Publishing Company. DO NOT DUPLICATE.

What People Think

Although Sarah was incorrect when she said that spiders and insects are the same thing, she was correct in saying that spiders and insects share many characteristics. This is one of the important tools that scientists use to classify organisms. They look at the similarities between two seemingly different organisms to find possible links. In fact, spiders and insects are related, since they are both **arthropods**, members of the phylum Arthropoda. However, Kendra makes a good point about classification: Even though both goldfish and humans are members of the phylum Chordata, no one would say, "Humans, goldfish—they're all the same to me!"

Classifying organisms is called *taxonomy*. You can think of a taxonomy as a model to help organize the amazing diversity of life. When it comes to classifying animals, some people have a very limited view of what an animal is, and they tend to classify animals according to a single characteristic, such as "number of legs." Scientists classify animals in terms of accepted biological characteristics, which often tend to be more abstract. Some of the characteristics that scientists use when classifying animals are structure (how they are built), function (how they do things), biochemical behavior (the chemistry of their bodies), nutritional needs (what they eat), embryonic development (how they grow), genetic structure (their living blueprint), and molecular makeup (what they are made of).

> Why is using these characteristics more effective than simply counting the number of legs an animal has?

_____

_____

_____

A Swedish scientist, Karolus Linnaeus, developed a classification system for living things in the 1700s. His hierarchical system involved grouping things into seven, increasingly similar groups—**kingdom**, **phylum**, **class**, **order**, **family**, **genus**, and **species**. This system has been modified to accommodate the greater understanding that scientists now have about characteristics of living things. In recent years, advances in DNA technology have helped scientists discover relations that they did not know existed before: For example, the giant panda has been shown to be related to bears, whereas earlier we thought they were relatives of the raccoon.

> Linnaeus's system originally had two kingdoms (Plantae and Animalia). What are the kingdoms in the current classification taxonomy?

_____

_____

© 2001 Buckle Down Publishing Company. DO NOT DUPLICATE.

Linnaeus used two-part Latin names to describe an organism's genus and species. Animals and plants that are very similar may have the same genus name but different species names. A tame cat is *Felis* (cat) *domesticus* (domestic), whereas a wild cat is *Felis sylvestris* (wild).

What are the Latin names (genus and species) for the following common organisms? (You will probably need to use a reference book or the Internet to find these and other scientific names for common organisms.)

People (human beings): _____

Pet dog: _____

Peach tree: _____

Scientists classify animals according to their internal and external structures, such as **vertebrates** (backbone) or **invertebrates** (no backbone). Invertebrates include arthropods, which have external skeletons and jointed appendages. Arthropods are divided into five classes: insects, millipedes, centipedes, arachnids, and crustaceans.

Vertebrates are members of the phylum Chordata. What are some major classes of chordates?

_____

_____

_____

An amoeba and a human are both animals. Give one reason why a human needs a **skeletal system** but an amoeba does not.

_____

_____

_____

In order to organize groups of animals into a classification system, scientists often must try to tell the difference between two very similar organisms. As you learned in Review 5, cells group together to form tissues, and tissues form organs. Organs also work together to form **organ systems**. One way scientists can classify very similar organisms is to look at how their internal organ systems function together. There are often tiny differences in these functions that help scientists classify animals. Let's look at some of the organ systems and how they relate in most animals.

© 2001 Buckle Down Publishing Company. DO NOT DUPLICATE.

The **respiratory system** and **circulatory system** depend on each other to function. The respiratory system brings oxygen into the body, and the circulatory system carries the oxygen to the body cells. The circulatory system also collects carbon dioxide (a waste product), and the respiratory system removes the waste carbon dioxide from the body.

How are the **digestive system** and **excretory system** related?

_____

_____

_____

Give another example of related body systems and explain how they are related.

_____

_____

_____

Control of other systems is carried out by the **endocrine system** and the **nervous system**. The endocrine system uses chemical hormones rather than nerve signals to control many body systems. These hormones are produced by glands in a person's body.

What are the effects of some common hormonal changes that occur in teenagers?

_____

_____

_____

The nervous system transmits electrical impulses throughout the body to control many body systems. The term *reaction time* refers to the amount of time it takes for your body systems to respond to something. If you are trying to catch a falling object, for example, your nerves, brain, and spinal cord are involved in controlling your muscular reaction.

Why is it impossible to have a reaction time equal to zero seconds?

_____

_____

_____

© 2001 Buckle Down Publishing Company. DO NOT DUPLICATE.

Using What You Know

You will need a magnifying lens, a plastic cup filled with water, a paper towel, an index card, and some wood bugs/pill bugs.

Step 1: Observe the bugs. Describe them.

_____

_____

_____

_____

Step 2: Place a bug in water for 10 seconds. Remove the bug, and place it on the paper towel. Describe what you see.

_____

_____

_____

_____

Step 3: Place the bugs on their backs. Observe them carefully. Describe what you see.

_____

_____

_____

_____

© 2001 Buckle Down Publishing Company. DO NOT DUPLICATE.

Think It Over

1. What class of arthropod is a pill bug? How do you know?

   _____

   _____

   _____

   _____

2. Were all the pill bugs from the same species?

   _____

   _____

   _____

   _____

3. Use the Internet to find out more about pill bugs. Record your findings on the lines below. Also include the Internet address you used.

   _____

   _____

   _____

   _____

© 2001 Buckle Down Publishing Company. DO NOT DUPLICATE.

Practice Questions

1. Mollusks often have hard shells. Why is this important to their survival?
   A. Shells are used to trap food.
   B. Shells make locomotion possible.
   C. Shells provide protection for their soft bodies.
   D. Shells make it possible for them to float in the ocean.

2. In multicellular organisms, groupings of specific parts within the organism are called *levels of organization*. Which of the following sequences is arranged in order from most complex to simplest?
   A. tissues, cells, organs, organ systems
   B. cells, tissues, organ systems, organs
   C. organs, cells, organ systems, tissues
   D. organ systems, organs, tissues, cells

3. Why are humans and bats both classified as mammals?
   A. Bats and humans interact with each other.
   B. Bats and humans share common characteristics.
   C. The sense organs of bats and humans are identical.
   D. Bats rely on humans for the food they need to survive.

4. Why is a taxonomy for living things important?
   A. It helps organize the diversity of life.
   B. It determines the characteristics of various animals.
   C. It is something that is constant and will never change.
   D. It tells you what organisms can be introduced to an environment.

5. You are ice skating with your friends. You look over your shoulder to see someone skating wildly, about to run into you. You feel your heart speed up, and you zip out of the way just in time. What are two of the organ systems that worked together to save you from a collision?
   A. digestive and skeletal
   B. endocrine and nervous
   C. circulatory and excretory
   D. respiratory and reproductive

© 2001 Buckle Down Publishing Company. DO NOT DUPLICATE.

Review 7
Life Cycles

A human begins life as a single, fertilized **egg** cell that eventually becomes an incredibly complex human organism. **Fertilization** is the first step in the life cycle that includes birth, growth, and death. You may be most familiar with life cycles in animals, but organisms such as plants have life cycles as well. Flowering plants have life cycles in which the seeds develop from the union of egg and **sperm** nuclei, and if conditions are favorable, the seeds grow into another generation of plants. This review will focus upon life cycles and reproduction in flowering plants and how certain systems work together in plants and in animals.

What Do You Think?

When you begin to think about the ways in which animals and flowering plants (which far outnumber nonflowering plants) go about the business of living, you will find that they both have common needs for living and surviving. This does not mean that flowering plants and animals meet those common needs in exactly the same way. Think about it this way: if you were planning a trip to New York City, you could choose any number of ways to get there. You could drive and choose from many roads. You could fly and have choices of airlines, times, and routes. You could even walk. (Well, maybe!) The bottom line is that you could accomplish this task in multiple ways. Similarly, plants and animals accomplish many of the same tasks in very different ways.

In the tables on the next page, some tasks are listed that both humans and flowering plants must carry out in order to stay alive and reproduce. You will fill in the tables to describe how these tasks are accomplished. (The first table is for humans; the second table is for flowering plants.) As you fill in the second table, remember that flowering plants are not free to get up and walk around (except in science fiction movies). As a result, they have developed various strategies to obtain food and to reproduce as they remain anchored in one place.

Key Words

anther

egg

fertilization

filament

genetic variability

ovary

ovule

petal

photosynthesis

pistil

pollination

respiration

sepal

sexual reproduction

sperm

stamen

stigma

style

© 2001 Buckle Down Publishing Company. DO NOT DUPLICATE.

In the table that follows, tell which organ systems help humans accomplish each function. There may be more than one system for each function.

Task	Human organ systems that help us do this
Energy intake	*digestive system*
Movement	
Transport of materials	
Control and coordination	
Body support	
Gas exchange	
Reproduction	

Now, use what you know about flowering plants to describe how you think they carry out each task.

Task	How I think a flowering plant does this
Energy intake	
Movement	
Transport of materials	
Control and coordination	
Body support	
Gas exchange	
Reproduction	

© 2001 Buckle Down Publishing Company. DO NOT DUPLICATE.

After finishing the tables, you probably noticed many ways that humans and plants accomplish similar life tasks and functions in different ways.

In nature, the survival of a species is of great importance, and reproduction is a critical piece in this survival. Why is reproduction so important to the survival of a species?

_____

_____

_____

What People Think

You are probably very familiar with the human life cycle, and you know that **sexual reproduction** is a vital element in this cycle. Sexual reproduction is also vital to the life cycle of flowering plants. In both humans and in flowering plants, sexual reproduction introduces **genetic variability**, which is important to species survival.

Flowering plants produce flowers, and, if the right events occur, these flowers produce seeds. If a seed lands in a place with favorable conditions, a new plant begins to grow.

The diagram below shows a typical flower. Consult an encyclopedia or a science textbook to complete this exercise. For this flower, label a **petal**, a **sepal**, a **stamen**, an **anther**, a **filament**, the **pistil**, the **ovary**, the **stigma**, and the **style**.

Parts of a Flower

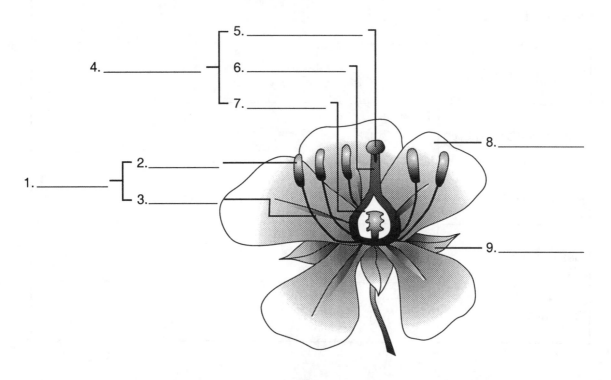

© 2001 Buckle Down Publishing Company. DO NOT DUPLICATE.

The male and female flower parts from the diagram are listed below. For each part, describe its role in the flower's reproduction.

Male Floral Parts

Stamen: _____

Anther: _____

Filament: _____

Female Floral Parts

Pistil: _____

Stigma: _____

Style: _____

Ovary: _____

Now that you know a bit about the anatomy of a flower, let's take a look at what must happen for a seed to be produced. One event that must take place is **pollination**. Pollen is the plant's male sex cell, or sperm. It has to be transferred from the stamens to the stigma of the flower. Some plants pollinate themselves, but cross-pollination is very common. In cross-pollination, pollen from one plant is carried to the stigma of another plant of the same species. The wind often takes care of this, but many plants depend on insects to transfer pollen.

If a plant species depends on insects to transfer pollen from the flowers of one plant to the flowers of another plant, what are two things that a flower might have to attract insects?

_____

_____

In flowering plants, pollination and fertilization are two different events. Even if pollen lands on the stigma, fertilization still has to occur. A sperm nucleus must join with an egg nucleus (the female sex cell) by making the "trip" from the stigma to an egg nucleus inside the **ovule**. For a seed to be produced, a sperm nucleus must unite with an egg nucleus.

© 2001 Buckle Down Publishing Company. DO NOT DUPLICATE.

The diagram that follows illustrates the anatomy of the female part (pistil) of the flower in the process of being fertilized by the male component. Label the following structures: pollen grain, pollen tube, **stigma**, **style**, **ovary**, and **ovule**.

Pistil
(Enlarged Longitudinal Section)

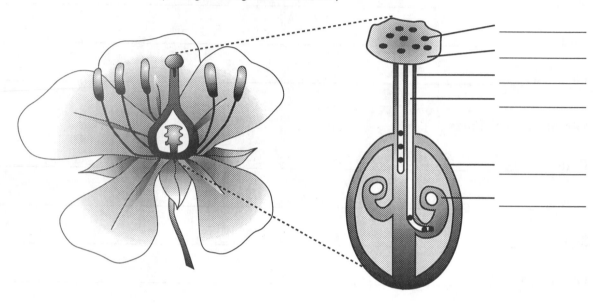

What advantage does a seed get from developing in and being surrounded by the plant ovary?

_____

_____

_____

After a seed matures into a fully grown plant, the plant begins to perform its most amazing function—creating the food that nourishes nearly all life on Earth. This function, called **photosynthesis**, is a chemical reaction that occurs in plants. Plants take in water and carbon dioxide and use the Sun's energy to produce oxygen and sugar:

$$\text{carbon dioxide} + \text{water} + \textit{sunlight} \rightarrow \text{oxygen} + \text{sugar}$$

Through this reaction, a plant essentially binds the Sun's energy in the form of sugar molecules. The plant can then store this energy. The plant stores some of the oxygen produced in photosynthesis, but it also releases some. Practically all of the oxygen in the Earth's atmosphere comes from photosynthetic reactions. The extraordinary benefits of photosynthesis are that a plant usually creates more oxygen and sugar than it needs, making these substances available to other organisms.

© 2001 Buckle Down Publishing Company. DO NOT DUPLICATE.

When a plant needs energy to grow, or when an animal eats the sugars contained in the plant, the stored energy is released through another chemical reaction, called **respiration**. Respiration occurs in all living things, including plants, allowing them to use the energy they get from food. This reaction takes oxygen and sugar and converts them into water, carbon dioxide, and energy. An organism then uses this energy to live and grow.

$$\text{oxygen} + \text{sugar} \rightarrow \text{carbon dioxide} + \text{water} + \textit{energy}$$

Have you noticed that respiration is basically photosynthesis in reverse? The most important result of these two reactions is that the Sun's energy has been changed into the energy that all living things need to survive. Photosynthesis produces materials that are required for respiration, and respiration produces materials that are required for photosynthesis. This is an example of materials cycling through the environment.

In the illustration below, fill in the blanks to show how you think photosynthesis and respiration work together to produce a cycle. Don't forget to identify all the materials needed and produced in the two chemical reactions.

Photosynthesis/Respiration Cycle

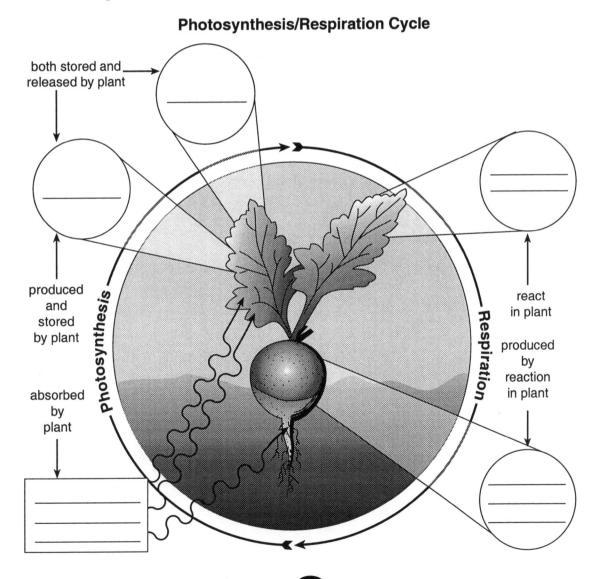

both stored and released by plant

produced and stored by plant

absorbed by plant

Photosynthesis

react in plant

produced by reaction in plant

Respiration

© 2001 Buckle Down Publishing Company. DO NOT DUPLICATE.

Using What You Know

In this activity, you will take a look at the internal structure of three fruits: an apple, a tomato, and a green bean. Each of the seeds inside these fruits has the potential to grow into a new plant. You will need a pencil to make labeled drawings of the apples, tomatoes, and green beans that have been set out in your classroom.

Station 1: One apple has been cut in a cross-section, and a second apple has been cut in a longitudinal section. Make a drawing of each section, and label a seed and the ovary.

How many chambers are there in the ovary of an apple?

_____

How many seeds were produced in the apple that was cut in a cross-section?

_____

© 2001 Buckle Down Publishing Company. DO NOT DUPLICATE.

Station 2: One tomato has been cut in a cross-section, and a second tomato has been cut in a longitudinal section. Make a drawing of each section, and label a seed and the ovary.

How does the structure inside the tomato differ from that of the apple? Does the tomato have a "core"?

_____

The apple is an example of a fruit type called a *pome*, and the tomato is an example of a fruit type that plant biologists call a *berry*.

Which fruit appears to produce more seeds, the tomato or the apple?

_____

For each seed that is produced, how many fertilizations have occurred?

_____

© 2001 Buckle Down Publishing Company. DO NOT DUPLICATE.

Station 3: While you might call a green bean a vegetable, it is actually a fruit, botanically speaking, since it is the seed-bearing organ of a plant. If someone has not already done so, split the pod open along the length of the pod. Make a drawing of the seed and pod. Label the pod, a seed, and an ovule.

How are the seeds (beans) arranged inside the pod? Do the beans appear to be attached to the wall of the pod in any way?

_____

_____

_____

Are all of the beans about the same size and equally developed?

_____

_____

Summary question: What are two characteristics shared by the apple, the tomato, and the green bean?

_____

_____

_____

© 2001 Buckle Down Publishing Company. DO NOT DUPLICATE.

Think It Over

1. Many flowering plants spend a great deal of energy producing fruits that are not only attractive but also energy-rich. Essentially, a plant sacrifices its own valuable energy to make the fruit. Why is fruit production so important to the ultimate survival of flowering plants?

_____

_____

_____

2. You may not think about something like an oak tree being a flowering plant, but those little acorns come from somewhere. If a flowering plant, like an oak, depends on the wind to carry its pollen, what is at least one difference that you would predict in the anatomy of wind-pollinated flowers as compared to insect-pollinated or self-pollinated flowers?

_____

_____

_____

3. Flowering plants produce many more seeds than you might think are necessary. What do you think is the main reason plants spend so much energy in seed production?

_____

_____

_____

4. Imagine this situation: A tremendous volcano has erupted, producing a dark cloud of ash and smoke that covers the entire North American continent, even extending into parts of South America. This cloud blocks out all sunlight for almost three months. What effects would you expect this disaster to have on the plants in the area? What about the other organisms?

_____

_____

_____

© 2001 Buckle Down Publishing Company. DO NOT DUPLICATE.

Practice Questions

Directions: Use the following diagram to answer Numbers 1 through 3.

Parts of a Flower

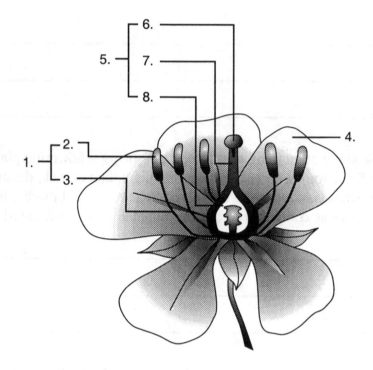

1. Which number corresponds to the place in the flower that produces pollen?

   A. 2

   B. 3

   C. 4

   D. 6

2. Which number corresponds to the part of the pistil where a seed could develop?

   A. 5

   B. 6

   C. 7

   D. 8

3. Which number corresponds to the part of the flower that typically becomes the fruit?

   A. 5

   B. 6

   C. 7

   D. 8

© 2001 Buckle Down Publishing Company. DO NOT DUPLICATE.

4. The sperm nuclei that fertilize egg nuclei develop from
   A. ovules.
   B. fruit.
   C. pollen grains.
   D. seeds.

5. What must green plants have in order for photosynthesis to take place?
   A. sunlight, oxygen, and water
   B. sunlight, carbon dioxide, and water
   C. sugar, water, and oxygen
   D. sunlight, carbon dioxide, and nutrient-rich soil

6. As you know, flowering plants grow in one place and are not free to move around like most animals. This means that plants have evolved with features that bring pollinators to them. This also means that plants have developed ways to have their seeds spread around.

   a) Describe two ways that plants attract pollinators.

   _____

   _____

   _____

   _____

   b) Describe two ways that seeds may be modified to help them spread.

   _____

   _____

   _____

   _____

© 2001 Buckle Down Publishing Company. DO NOT DUPLICATE.

Review 8
Reproduction and Heredity

While watching ESPN with a friend, you wonder what it would be like to play in the NBA. Your friend says that when he gets to college, he will be 6'10" and will surely be a first-round draft pick. Your friend is 5'3" today. Neither his mother nor his father is much taller. You have a general idea about the average height of professional basketball players. Do you think your friend will ever see his name on an NBA roster?

In this review, we will take a look at how traits are passed along from parents to offspring through reproduction and heredity. You also will learn about how our cells begin their development during the earliest stages of life.

What Do You Think?

Heredity is the passing of **traits** from parents to offspring. **Genetics** is the study of how traits are inherited.

Explain how heredity occurs. You can use words, pictures, or both in your explanation.

Key Words

asexual reproduction

chromosome

DNA

dominant trait

embryo

fertilization

gamete

gene

genetics

heredity

meiosis

mitosis

nucleus

recessive trait

reproduction

sexual reproduction

trait

variation

zygote

© 2001 Buckle Down Publishing Company. DO NOT DUPLICATE.

What People Think

Reproduction involves the creation of an entire organism. Reproduction can occur by two different means, asexual or sexual. In **asexual reproduction**, the offspring has only one parent. In this kind of reproduction, a single plant multiplies without the aid of seeds, sex cells (egg and sperm), or **fertilization**, the process in which an egg and sperm unite to begin the growth of a new organism. For example, some types of algae reproduce asexually by **mitosis**; portions simply break off the parent plant, and the cells divide to create new offspring.

More complex plants, such as strawberry plants, also can reproduce asexually by sending out runners, or small vines, from the parent plant. Offspring of asexual reproduction are clones of the single adult parent. Although the strawberry plant produces seed by means of sexual reproduction (the seeds are visible on the strawberry fruit), new plants are also created by runners sent out from the adult plant. These runners anchor to the soil with small roots, forming tiny plants at these locations. The growth of the new plants occurs through cell division, a process in which the **chromosomes** of the individual cells are duplicated and separated on opposite sides of the cell. Chromosomes are threadlike strands of **DNA** that carry a code telling what traits the organism will have. A cell membrane then forms between the two sets of identical and complete chromosomes. The new cells are copies of the original cells. These cells may develop into stems, leaves, or roots. As a new plant develops and grows, it continues to be supported by the adult plant. Once the new plant becomes self-sufficient—with green leaves, stem, and complete root system—the runner dies, separating the new plant from its single adult parent.

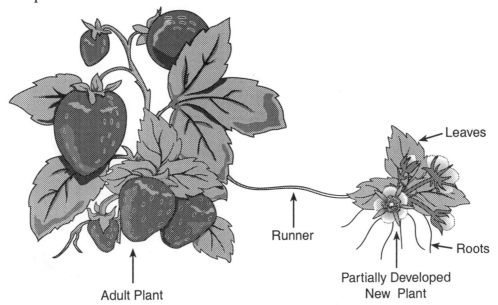

Leaves

Runner

Roots

Adult Plant

Partially Developed
New Plant

Some types of flowers and fruits are cultivated using asexual reproduction. For example, certain orchid plants are reproduced by growing small pieces cut from the parent plant. What is an advantage of this kind of reproduction?

_____

_____

© 2001 Buckle Down Publishing Company. DO NOT DUPLICATE.

In contrast to the offspring of asexual reproduction, offspring of **sexual reproduction** have two parents. A sperm cell from one parent and an egg cell from the other parent are combined through fertilization. Sexual reproduction results in offspring that have genetic material from both parents. These offspring may have some characteristics (traits) of each parent. They might also inherit characteristics from their parents that aren't visible in their parents but are nonetheless present.

An organism's genetic information is stored in the control center of the cell, the **nucleus**. The nucleus of a human cell contains 46 chromosomes. The code for each type of trait (for example, eye color) is carried in separate **genes** on the chromosomes. The sperm and egg (or **gametes**) each contain only 23 chromosomes. Why do gametes have only half as many chromosomes as other cells? Human gametes are produced in the reproductive organs of the parents through a process known as **meiosis**. Through meiosis, a gamete only contains half the regular number of chromosomes, 23. When fertilization occurs, 23 chromosomes from one parent are joined to the 23 chromosomes of the other parent, for a total of 46.

Complete the following diagrams of an organism that normally has eight chromosomes reproducing by asexual and sexual means.

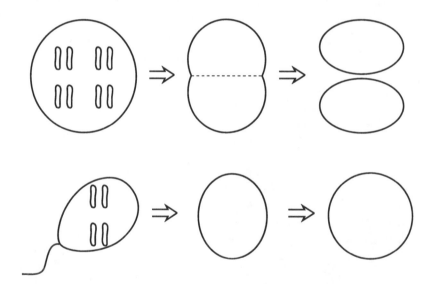

© 2001 Buckle Down Publishing Company. DO NOT DUPLICATE.

Through sexual reproduction, the new organism receives half of its chromosomes from one parent and half from the other. Because of this, the offspring receives two genes for each trait. For example, the parents each pass on a gene for hair color. Sometimes the parents will pass on the same gene, and sometimes they will each pass on a different one. The **dominant trait** is the trait that appears in an offspring when two different genes are mixed; the **recessive trait** is the one that does not appear when two different genes are mixed.

How can two dark-eyed and dark-haired parents have blue-eyed and blond-haired offspring?

_____

_____

_____

In sexual reproduction, the egg and sperm unite to form a single cell called a **zygote**. As the fertilized egg cell divides (undergoes mitosis), it grows and develops into an **embryo**.

Zygote Formation

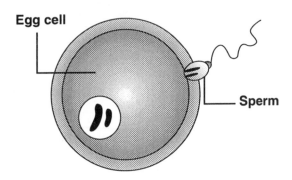

During the embryo's development, the DNA in the nucleus of each cell directs it to form a specific type of tissue. The DNA instructs some cells to be muscle cells, others to be brain cells, and so on.

Of course, our cells continue to develop even after we are born. As we get older, our bones, muscles, and other tissues grow. Meanwhile, many of our old, worn-out cells are replaced by new ones.

© 2001 Buckle Down Publishing Company. DO NOT DUPLICATE.

Using What You Know

In this activity, you will explore the different genetic traits found in your family.

Step 1: List members of your family in the far left column of the following chart, starting with yourself.

Family Member	Hair Color	Eye Color	Earlobes Attached?
Me			

Step 2: Describe the physical characteristics of each person listed in the chart.

Step 3: Which, if any, of these characteristics can change naturally in a person over time?

_____

_____

_____

Think It Over

1. Differences in the traits of parents and offspring are called **variations**. What variations did you find in your family chart?

_____

_____

© 2001 Buckle Down Publishing Company. DO NOT DUPLICATE.

2. The following model shows a genetic pattern that begins with Mr. A and Ms. B. Darker-shaded shapes in the model indicate people who have earlobes that are not attached, which is a dominant trait. Lighter shaded shapes indicate people who have attached earlobes, a recessive trait.

The following genetics model shows that Mr. A (*square*) and Ms. B (*circle*) had two male children, D and E. The male child E gets married to Ms. G, and Mr. E and Ms. G have a female child, K.

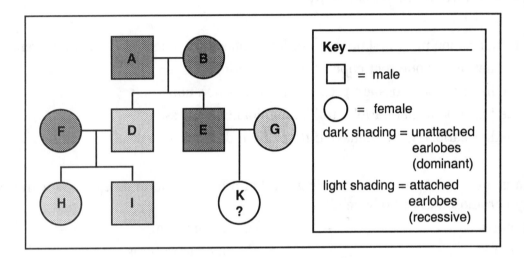

For each trait, an offspring receives one gene from the mother and one from the father. This means that the offspring is then able to pass on only one of those genes in reproduction. Note that Mr. D and Ms. F had two children with attached earlobes.

List the possible earlobe gene combinations for the people listed below. Record your answers in terms of dominant and recessive genes.

Mr. A: _____

Ms. B: _____

Mr. D: _____

Ms. F: _____

3. Does K have attached or unattached earlobes? _____

What is the reason for your answer? _____

_____

_____

© 2001 Buckle Down Publishing Company. DO NOT DUPLICATE.

Practice Questions

1. Genetics is the study of
   A. a person's family tree.
   B. how traits are inherited.
   C. food and how the body uses it.
   D. the structures of the human body.

2. What information must be known in order to make inferences about earlobe genes?
   A. whether an earlobe trait appears in an offspring
   B. whether earlobe genes are present in every generation
   C. whether a particular earlobe trait is dominant or recessive
   D. whether earlobe genes behave differently in different people

3. What is the special process of cell division that produces sperm or egg cells with half as many chromosomes as body cells?
   A. mitosis   C. metabolism
   B. meiosis   D. metamorphosis

4. What is the best way to know for sure what kinds of genes a person has?
   A. Test the person's blood and analyze the DNA.
   B. List the person's physical traits in a detailed chart.
   C. Ask the person about the traits his/her parents or children have.
   D. Make a family-tree model of all the person's known ancestors and their traits.

5. You know that variation in a species produces offspring that have some traits that are different from their parents' traits. Perhaps a bird's beak is a slightly different shape from its parents' beaks, or a cat's ears are somehow different from its parents' ears. How might variations help organisms survive?

   _____

   _____

   _____

   _____

   _____

© 2001 Buckle Down Publishing Company. DO NOT DUPLICATE.

Review 9
Evolution

Whether you realize it or not, your family history goes back to the beginning of humankind. The search for your "roots" (the people who were your ancestors) is called *genealogy*. It's a kind of puzzle in which you piece together facts about the family members who came before you. Learning about your ancestors can also show how you came to have the physical traits you have. In your research, you may find that your chin, with its huge dimple, is exactly like your father's grandfather's chin. Or maybe you find that the cowlick you find so annoying on the left side of your hair is a trait shared by your mother and your grandmother and your grandmother's father. Common threads run through the generations of families.

The group of characteristics that makes up your physical body is a product of your **heredity**. You didn't get that dimpled chin and cowlick from just anywhere: they were handed down to you through the genetic material of your ancestors. Scientists who study **evolution** engage in a kind of genetic puzzle-solving as they piece together clues about the origins of all living things. This review will discuss some of the current scientific thoughts about evolution.

What Do You Think?

The study of genealogy is limited by human memory and recorded history, but that's not the case with the study of evolution. Although no one can know for certain how life on Earth developed or how it came to have so much variation, scientists have collected evidence that has allowed them to propose several different models.

Before England's Industrial Age, light-colored moths were far more common than dark-colored moths. These moths were a food source for birds. During the Industrial Revolution, a great amount of coal was burned in factories, resulting in severe air pollution. Gradually, observers noticed increasing numbers of dark moths and fewer light moths. What is a possible reason for this change in the numbers of dark- and light-colored moths?

_____

_____

_____

_____

Key Words

adaptation

coevolution

evolution

heredity

natural selection

paleontologist

© 2001 Buckle Down Publishing Company. DO NOT DUPLICATE.

As other kinds of fuel were used in England, a decrease in coal burning resulted in less pollution and less dark soot. In time, what would you expect to happen to the numbers of light and dark moths? Give a reason to support your thinking.

_____

_____

_____

_____

What People Think

The changes attributed to evolution take generations of species to appear. The process of **natural selection** is often used to explain how organisms change over time. Usually, organisms of a species vary in their genetic makeup. To confirm this, you could look at the range of physical features in your friends. If you were to look at all organisms, you might notice that some of them have certain traits that improve their chances of survival. If certain members of a species have a trait that increases their chances of surviving, those members are more likely to reproduce; in turn, those varieties without the trait tend to become less numerous. Over time, this process produces organisms adapted to survive in a specific environment.

Imagine that you are observing a population of cheetahs. Some are very slow runners, and some are very fast runners. If you are a cheetah, you must chase antelope for your dinner, and the slowest antelopes can outrun the slowest cheetahs. Which group of cheetahs do you think has the survival advantage? Why?

_____

_____

Which group of antelope has the best survival chances? Why?

_____

_____

In both the cheetah and the antelope populations, what **adaptation** do you think is being naturally selected? Why?

_____

_____

© 2001 Buckle Down Publishing Company. DO NOT DUPLICATE.

Life in the wild is more complex than the previous cheetah-antelope example; many variables interact in the process of natural selection. Gradual climate changes can cause certain traits to become dominant, like the thicker fur that polar bears developed during the last Ice Age. Humans have become the dominant species on Earth, and so we have gained the power to change the environment much more quickly and drastically than usually occurs in nature. What happens when the environment changes so rapidly? Let's look at an example.

Salmon return to the Snake River each year and swim upstream to the point where they were hatched to spawn (lay their eggs and reproduce). Dams have been placed in the Snake River to control the river. The courses of rivers usually take thousands of years to change, but now they can be drastically altered practically overnight.

Explain one way you think this has affected the survival of the salmon population.

_____

_____

What is one course of action that could be taken to help the salmon population survive?

_____

_____

Because bacteria and insects have very short life cycles and produce many offspring, they can provide evolutionary evidence in a relatively short time. This information is important to scientists who are working to develop antibiotics and pesticides, as well as those studying evolution in general. For example, a scientist could test a pesticide on a population of fruit flies, and she would be able to observe the effects of the chemical on multiple generations within a year. The same number of generations in a population of mice would take many years.

If you get a bacterial infection and go to a doctor, you may get a prescription for an antibiotic, a medicine designed to kill the kind of bacteria that is making you sick. However, not all of the bacteria will die. Even bacteria of the same species are not genetically identical. Some may have genes that make them resistant to that antibiotic.

If you were to continue to use an antibiotic over a long period of time, what would happen to its effectiveness against the type of bacteria that it was supposed to fight?

_____

_____

_____

© 2001 Buckle Down Publishing Company. DO NOT DUPLICATE.

Explain how the use of antibiotics actually helps nature select for antibiotic-resistant strains of bacteria.

_____

_____

_____

What do antibiotic-resistant bacteria demonstrate about genetic variation within species?

_____

_____

Evolution is a controversial topic. One reason for this controversy is the belief of some people that the scientific theory of evolution is at odds with religious teachings and beliefs. In contrast, other people believe that the controversy between science and religion is counterproductive, since science is based on evidence in nature, and religion is based on faith. Both provide valuable perspective on our universe.

Scientists believe that their studies of the natural record are evidence for evolution. What kinds of evidence do scientists use to arrive at the conclusion that species have changed over time?

_____

_____

_____

The skeletal structure of many mammals' forelimbs is practically identical, bone for bone. This similarity includes species as different as rats, dogs, humans, bats, horses, and porpoises. The clearest and simplest explanation for this is that all these species share a common ancestor. When scientists want to show how this similarity could remain throughout millions of years of evolution, they often point to the fossil evidence for the evolution of horses. The eohippus, or "dawn horse," lived about 55 million years ago. It stood less than 1 meter high and had three soft toes instead of a hoof. **Paleontologists**, scientists who bridge the gap between geology and biology, have traced a very clear line of relationship between the eohippus and the modern horse. Although the modern horse has a much more complex brain, a larger size, and a different toe structure (a hoof), it still shows the forelimb structure of the eohippus.

© 2001 Buckle Down Publishing Company. DO NOT DUPLICATE.

Evolution of the Modern Horse

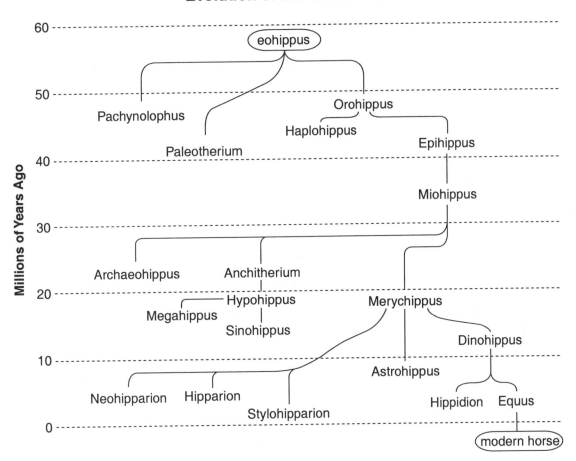

If the eohippus evolved into the modern horse, why do you think it also gave rise to so many other types of prehistoric horses that became extinct?

_____

_____

When a gene in an individual organism mutates (changes), that mutation has the potential to create variety in the species. If the mutation results in a successful trait (one that increases the organism's chance of survival), that trait is likely to be passed on to offspring. If the new trait is unsuccessful (one that decreases the organism's chance of survival), the organism is less likely to live long enough to mate and produce offspring. In this way, the presence of the unsuccessful trait in the gene pool is diminished. If there are no offspring, the altered gene cannot be passed on. Even if the organism with an unsuccessful trait does mate, the survival of its offspring is questionable.

Why is sexual reproduction a source of variation in organisms?

_____

_____

© 2001 Buckle Down Publishing Company. DO NOT DUPLICATE.

Using What You Know

Charles Darwin traveled to the Galápagos Islands and formed conclusions based upon his observations of the plants and animals he saw on his trip. You, too, have made observations about the natural world. You've no doubt noticed that birds' beaks and feet vary widely among different species. A duck's webbed feet and rounded bill, for example, are much different than a hawk's curved beak and taloned feet. These variations aren't just interesting differences; they are adaptations that have developed over much time and many generations to help the species survive.

In the following activity, you'll explore the connection between the shape of a bird's beak or bill and the food that it eats. Your teacher will assign some students to play the role of birds and will give further directions. During the activity, record your observations in the following table.

Trial 1		Trial 2	
Type of Beak	Kinds of Foods Picked Up	Type of Beak	Kinds of Foods Picked Up

What happened when some of the food types were removed completely?

_____

_____

_____

If the food supplies for these birds is not restored, what prediction can you make about the future population of the different species? Explain.

_____

_____

_____

© 2001 Buckle Down Publishing Company. DO NOT DUPLICATE.

Think It Over

1. How is the structure of each "beak" related to the properties of the "food" that it was best able to pick up?

   _____

   _____

2. Think about all of the variations in the structure of birds' beaks, bodies, and feet. These are adaptations that have survival value for the species. These adaptations vary with the habitat or environment in which the bird lives. This is an example of how organisms diversify. Insects also exhibit extensive variation. Describe two examples of adaptations in insects that have survival value for what the insect does.

   _____

   _____

   _____

3. Many flowering plants are pollinated by insects or birds. Over time, flower structure and certain structures of the pollinator coevolve. For example, hummingbirds and the flowers from which they collect nectar provide an example of **coevolution**. How is the shape of a hummingbird's beak related to the shape of these flowers?

   _____

   _____

4. Bats and most birds can fly. However, the bat is a mammal, and the bird is not. This is an example of evolution where a condition of the habitat (in this case, the need to take to the air to catch food) has caused very different animals to develop similar traits. Sharks and dolphins both live in the ocean, but they are very different kinds of animals in terms of classification. How are sharks and dolphins alike, and how are they different?

   Alike: _____

   _____

   Different: _____

   _____

© 2001 Buckle Down Publishing Company. DO NOT DUPLICATE.

Practice Questions

Directions: Each of the rectangles in the following illustrations represents a different environment. Study the illustrations, then answer Number 1.

1. Which "creature" below would have the best chance of surviving in one of these environments?

A.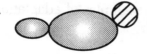

C.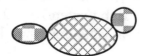

B.

D.

2. Which of the following would be the least convincing evidence to support evolution?
   A. similarities in embryonic development among present-day animals
   B. similarities in DNA among fossil animals and present-day animals
   C. similarities in DNA among fossil plants and present-day plants
   D. similarities in behaviors among a group of present-day animals

3. Finches living on the relatively small group of Galápagos Islands have great variation in beak structures. Describe how these variations occurred over time.

_____

_____

_____

_____

_____

_____

_____

© 2001 Buckle Down Publishing Company. DO NOT DUPLICATE.

Directions: Use the following illustrations of birds' feet to answer Numbers 4 and 5.

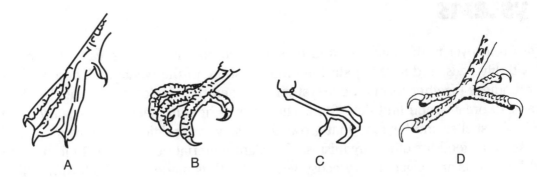

A   B   C   D

4. What is the best explanation for the variety of birds' feet shown?
   A. They have evolved as a result of successful variations.
   B. They represent stages in the evolution of webbed feet.
   C. They are feet of birds that evolved from different species.
   D. They are feet of the same type of bird at different stages in life.

5. Which of the birds' feet shown is best adapted for walking over muddy ground?
   A. A   C. C
   B. B   D. D

PEOPLE IN SCIENCE

Charles Darwin
(England 1809–1882)

Charles Darwin studied plant and animal life. He is famous for coming up with the idea that all animals, including man, developed from life forms that lived millions of years ago. We call his idea *the theory of evolution.* Darwin spent five years on a boat at sea working on his ideas. He was very unhappy; he was seasick all the time. When his trip ended, Darwin decided he would never travel again. Instead, he married, had 10 children, and took only short vacations within Great Britain. He did all his scientific study at home, using the information and materials he had collected during his sea voyage. He built a large house with a large study and designed a special microscope. For the first eight years, he studied only barnacles. When his children were young, he once said they thought all fathers worked at home and studied barnacles. At another time in his life, he decided to study earthworms. For a while, he even kept live worms on top of the piano. He liked to watch the worms' activity when the piano was played. Darwin published many books about his research. His most famous book is *On the Origin of Species*, which explains his theory of evolution.

© 2001 Buckle Down Publishing Company. DO NOT DUPLICATE.

Review 10
Ecosystems

A large fish rolls over in the shallows, a turtle suns itself on a rock, frogs leap into a pool covered with lily pads, and herons patrol the muddy shore of the wetlands. These animals and their surroundings together form an **ecosystem**. The heron looks for fish to eat. The fish swim in the water to breathe and find their food. The water is held in place by clay subsoil. The turtle looks for shelter and for food that grows in these wet conditions. The frogs search for food and serve as food for other organisms. The plant material decomposes to form nutrient-rich food for insects and algae. Every ecosystem on Earth is made up of both **biotic** (living) and **abiotic** (nonliving) factors that enable the species that live there to survive and **adapt** to the ecosystem's unique conditions.

What Do You Think?

The living components of an environment constantly interact with the nonliving components. Plants, for example, interact with the Sun when they use **phototropism**, the tendency of plants to bend or lean toward light in order to get the most energy for photosynthesis. Adapting to the nonliving factors in the ecosystem, like sunlight and climate, is vital for living things to survive. When ice, snow, and colder temperatures arrive in an ecosystem in winter, many plants and animals go into a state of **dormancy** in order to conserve energy until warmer weather returns. These sorts of adaptations develop over long periods of time and many generations of the organism.

Describe at least two ways that organisms living in a desert ecosystem interact with abiotic factors in order to survive.

_____

_____

_____

_____

Describe at least two ways that organisms living in an oak forest ecosystem interact with biotic factors in order to survive.

_____

_____

_____

Key Words

abiotic

adapt

biodiversity

biome

biotic

catastrophic disturbance

dormancy

dynamic equilibrium

ecology

ecosystem

food chain

phototropism

succession

© 2001 Buckle Down Publishing Company. DO NOT DUPLICATE.

What are some changes that happen in the oak forest ecosystem in winter?

_____

_____

_____

What People Think

Ecology is the study of natural environmental systems. People have observed that, when left alone, all living and nonliving things on the planet interact in ways that create a living balance, or **dynamic equilibrium**. Keeping an equilibrium helps to maintain stable populations over thousands of years.

Balance is the key to species survival. For example, when too many predators are located in the same area, the prey species become so scarce that the predators often die from starvation. On the other hand, when no predators exist, species that are usually prey get overpopulated and can also starve from too great a demand placed on their food supply. Furthermore, overpopulation increases the chances of diseases within a population.

Maintaining balance in ecosystems is essential for humans, too. Every day, humans depend on biotic and abiotic factors to meet our daily needs. Although you may not think about it, the gas in the car or bus that delivers you to school or to the store comes from oil, a fossil fuel which was made from dead plants and animals. The cotton shirt you are wearing and the paper you write on come from plants. The hamburgers that people eat come from an animal, but that animal eats plants. Some of the plant and animal materials that we use every day might not be so obvious.

Think of examples of plant, animal, and nonliving things that benefit you. Use the categories in the table below to record your examples. If you are unsure of an example, leave it blank for now.

Use	Plant Example	Animal Example	Nonliving Thing Example
Food			
Fuel			
Household products			
Raw materials for making things			

© 2001 Buckle Down Publishing Company. DO NOT DUPLICATE.

An ecosystem can go through major changes because of natural causes or, quite often, human activities. For example, wolves once roamed the meadows and forests of Michigan, but hunting and habitat destruction by humans have mostly eliminated them from the state. The wolves had kept the deer population in control, but now that they're gone, humans must keep the deer from overpopulation and starvation. Anyone who lives in rural Michigan (or even some suburbs) can describe the problems that result from deer overpopulation. Many states now have regulated hunting seasons and state-organized deer kills to take the place of the wolves in maintaining the ecological balance of the ecosystem.

If a predator relies on a certain type of bird for food, what will the predator do if this bird species migrates each winter?

_____

_____

_____

There are always limits on the size of any population of plants or animals. Many of these limits relate to variations in the weather from year to year. For example, "bad" winters with unusually heavy snowfall and extremely low temperatures reduce the population of deer in an area. Balance in an ecosystem is achieved when the positive growth of a population is roughly equal to the negative effects of predators and climate.

Large geographic areas containing several separate ecosystems exist in North America and other parts of the world. These large geographic areas are called **biomes**. A biome has a characteristic climate and vegetation that is adapted to that climate. Examples of biomes include coniferous forests, deciduous forests, tropical rain forests, deserts, tundra, grasslands, savannas, woodlands, and chaparral. Each biome supports specific communities of well-adapted plants, animals, fungi, and microscopic creatures. The healthiest biomes are those with the greatest **biodiversity**, or variety in the types of organisms that live there.

Describe how plants and animals in the biome in which you live are affected by the changes in the seasons.

_____

_____

_____

© 2001 Buckle Down Publishing Company. DO NOT DUPLICATE.

Change in a biome is inevitable, and good biodiversity helps ensure that a biome can survive whatever changes come its way. This is done through a process called **succession**, in which plant and animal populations are slowly replaced over time by different plant and animal populations. For example, if you visited a large pond that had a few young trees around it, you would find large fish in the water, lots of bushes and undergrowth, and water plants. After about 50 years, you would find a marsh or a bog: Rain and streams have carried eroded materials into the pond, and plant and animal organisms have died and fallen to the floor of the pond. This activity has made the pond extremely shallow. The trees provide more shade, so there is less ground cover. Turtles are now the dominant species. If you returned in 100 years, you might find that the marsh has disappeared completely, turning the area back to a deciduous forest.

Using a reference book, describe an instance of naturally occurring ecological succession that occurs in the biome in which you live.

_____

_____

_____

All living things on our planet Earth must get food in some way to survive. As you learned in Review 7, plants use sunlight, water, and carbon dioxide from the atmosphere to make their own food through photosynthesis: This is the source of all food energy on Earth, with a few strange exceptions (see page 183). There are countless examples of **food chains** all over the world, but if you picked any one of them, you would find that they all rely on the Sun's energy.

Food chains can adapt to regular weather variations, but unexpected events, called **catastrophic disturbances**, also occur from time to time. The 1980 eruption of Mount St. Helens in Washington is an example of a catastrophic disturbance. This eruption caused major changes in the surrounding ecosystems of the conifer forest biome.

How might a year in which many new grasses grow in a grassland ecosystem help the population of snakes increase?

_____

_____

_____

_____

© 2001 Buckle Down Publishing Company. DO NOT DUPLICATE.

What would you expect to happen if the primary food source of an organism were destroyed by a catastrophic event in the ecosystem?

_____

_____

_____

How could a long-term climate change—over the course of 10,000 years, for example— affect an ecosystem?

_____

_____

_____

PEOPLE IN SCIENCE

Jane Goodall
(Great Britain 1934–)

Jane Goodall knew as a child in Great Britain that her life's work would be with animals. She loved to read animal books and study animals in nature. At age 23, she went to Africa to work with Dr. Louis Leakey. Dr. Leakey was a famous anthropologist (a person who studies the physical and cultural backgrounds of humans), and Goodall assisted Dr. Leakey in his search for fossils of early humans. Later, Dr. Leakey suggested that Goodall work with live chimpanzees. Dr. Goodall found her career with that assignment. Her study of chimpanzees who live near Lake Tanganyika in what is now Tanzania is the longest continuous study of animals in their natural surroundings. Goodall discovered that chimps are complex, intelligent creatures with rich emotional lives. They have unique personalities. They also use tools and hunt in ways similar to humans. Today, Goodall travels the world, speaking about the importance of all life on this planet. She has helped raise human understanding of other animal life forms.

© 2001 Buckle Down Publishing Company. DO NOT DUPLICATE.

Using What You Know

In this activity, you will use what you know about biomes to study three different biomes on Earth. Below are photographs of a tropical rain forest biome, the Arctic tundra biome, and a grassland biome.

Study the photos below, then describe the abiotic and biotic characteristics of each biome.

Tropical rain forest:

Abiotic: _____

_____

Biotic: _____

_____

Arctic tundra:

Abiotic: _____

_____

Biotic: _____

_____

Grassland:

Abiotic: _____

_____

Biotic: _____

_____

© 2001 Buckle Down Publishing Company. DO NOT DUPLICATE.

Think It Over

1. Many of the great grasslands in North America have been made into farms. What effects has this had on the biodiversity of the prairies?

   _____

   _____

   _____

2. The tropical rain forests of South America are being cut down for lumber and mining. What effect does this have on tropical birds?

   _____

   _____

   _____

3. How do tundra birds and mammals respond to the differences between Arctic summers and winters?

   _____

   _____

   _____

4. What adaptations in the structure of Arctic plants allow them to survive?

   _____

   _____

   _____

© 2001 Buckle Down Publishing Company. DO NOT DUPLICATE.

Practice Questions

Directions: Caribou live in the tundra biome in the far northern areas of the world. They move from place to place each fall and spring so that they are always near a food source. The following diagram represents the yearly movements of a giant herd of caribou over many kilometers. Use this information to answer Number 1.

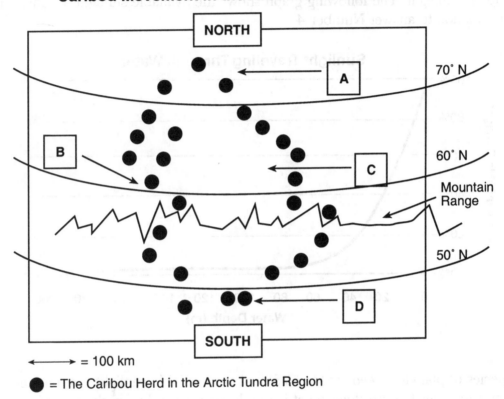

Caribou Movement in the Arctic Tundra Biome

NORTH

70° N
A
B
60° N
C
Mountain Range
50° N
D

SOUTH

←——→ = 100 km

● = The Caribou Herd in the Arctic Tundra Region

1. Where would you expect the caribou to be in January?

   A. A

   B. B

   C. C

   D. D

2. Which adaptation would best fit a plant that lives in a desert biome?

   A. having long roots

   B. growing very tall and green

   C. producing large amounts of juicy fruit

   D. attracting more herbivores than its competitors

© 2001 Buckle Down Publishing Company. DO NOT DUPLICATE.

3. Which of the following shows an effect of seasonal change on animals in a biome?

   A. wolves chasing deer

   B. seals trying to escape a shark attack

   C. animals digging in the mud for food

   D. animals migrating from north to south

Directions: Plankton are tiny organisms that must live near the surface of their marine biome home to capture sunlight. The following graph shows the available sunlight at different depths. Use this information to answer Number 4.

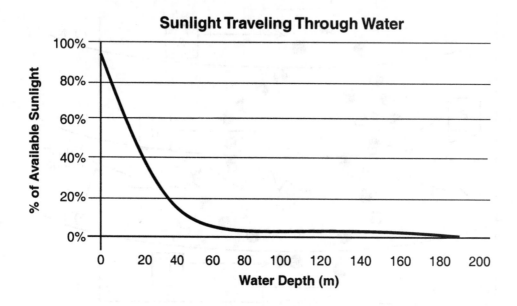

4. If a species of plankton needs at least 75% of the available sunlight that hits the surface of the water in order to reproduce, what is the deepest it can live in the water?

   A. about 8 m

   B. about 35 m

   C. about 55 m

   D. about 200 m

5. Sally planted an ivy plant and placed the pot on her windowsill. After a few weeks, she noticed it growing toward the sunlight coming through her window. This is an example of

   A. geotropism.

   B. phototropism.

   C. photosynthesis.

   D. solar gravitation.

© 2001 Buckle Down Publishing Company. DO NOT DUPLICATE.

unit 3

Physical Science

© 2001 Buckle Down Publishing Company. DO NOT DUPLICATE.

Review 11
Properties of Matter

There are some pretty amazing materials in the world today. For example, people living at the beginning of the 20th century would be astounded to see zippered plastic bags, lightweight aluminum metals, and nylon stockings. If you analyze all of these materials, however, you will find that every single one is made from the limited number of **elements** in our world. Read on to learn more about these tiny building blocks of **matter**.

What Do You Think?

Everything in the universe is made of matter, but not all types of matter have the same **properties**. To put it another way, different things act in different ways.

On the lines below, create a definition for the term *matter*.

_____

_____

_____

Think about a basketball and a watermelon. What are some properties that these two items have in common?

_____

_____

_____

What are some properties that make each of these items unique?

_____

_____

_____

Key Words

atom

density

element

graduated cylinder

mass

matter

phase

physical change

property

temperature

volume

© 2001 Buckle Down Publishing Company. DO NOT DUPLICATE.

What People Think

Matter takes up space and has mass—two qualities that we can measure. There are other features of matter that we can measure as well. We can find out the **temperature** of an object. We can also describe an object by how it looks. Is it a solid or a liquid or a gas? Is it smooth or bumpy? Later in this review, we will see that the arrangement of the atoms that make up matter dictates the way it looks and behaves.

Matter can exist in four different states called **phases**. When matter changes from one phase to another, the transformation is called a **physical change**. The chemical composition of the matter is the same in each phase, but the matter changes in appearance. The four phases of matter are as follows:

- solid, in which matter has a definite shape and volume
- liquid, in which matter has definite volume but no definite shape
- gas, in which matter has neither a definite shape nor volume
- plasma, which is like the gas phase except that the matter can conduct electricity and be affected by a magnetic field

There are more than 100 different elements. An element is any material that is made up of a single type of **atom**. All matter on Earth is made up of one or more of the elements.

What are some elements you know of? What state of matter are they at room temperature?

_____

_____

_____

Water is a type of matter made up of two elements—hydrogen and oxygen. Water exists as a liquid, solid, and gas. One interesting property of water that makes it so important for life is that it exists in all three phases at temperatures that regularly occur on Earth.

Imagine that you have a solid block of ice, and you need to measure its temperature, volume, and mass. How would you go about this task?

_____

_____

_____

© 2001 Buckle Down Publishing Company. DO NOT DUPLICATE.

To measure an object's **volume**, you can use a ruler or meterstick, depending on the size of the object. For rectangular objects, like a block, volume can be found by measuring length, width, and height and multiplying them together. The metric units of measurement include millimeters (mm), centimeters (cm), meters (m), and kilometers (km). Small objects, such as a book, are measured in millimeters or centimeters; medium-sized objects, such as a room, will be measured in meters; and large objects or distances, such as the distance across Lake Huron, are measured in kilometers. When you multiply your measurements together to find volume, they all must be the same unit. For example, a block with the dimensions 3 m × 3 m × 4 m would have a volume of 36 m³, cubic meters. The fact that the units are cubed shows three-dimensional volume measurement. A measure in regular meters would indicate a measurement of length (one dimension), and a measure in square meters (m²) would indicate a measurement of area (two dimensions).

What's the volume of a block of ice measuring 2 cm × 3 cm × 2 cm?

_____

A thermometer is used to measure the temperature of a substance. Two units used to measure temperature are Celsius (C) and Fahrenheit (F). These are simply two different scales for measuring the same thing. Both of these temperature scales have common reference points—the freezing temperature of pure water (0° C and 32° F) and the boiling temperature of pure water (100° C and 212° F).

As you know, you can measure the length of an object in centimeters or inches. If you measure in both units, you will get two different numbers with different units. The results look different but actually represent the same thing: 1 inch is equivalent to 2.54 cm. Similarly, you can measure time in seconds or minutes. Although the answers look different, 1.5 minutes is identical to 90 seconds. The same thing holds true when you are measuring temperature with Celsius or Fahrenheit thermometers. This helps us understand why units are so important. Before you stick your hand in 70° water, you'd better find out what unit was used!

To convert between Celsius and Fahrenheit, use the following formula.

$$T_{Fahr} = \frac{9}{5} T_{Cels} + 32$$

Rewrite the formula in the form T_{Cels} = _____. Show your work.

_____

_____

© 2001 Buckle Down Publishing Company. DO NOT DUPLICATE.

If a block of ice has a temperature of 25° F, what is its temperature in Celsius?

_____

_____

Mass can be found by using a balance or a scale. Mass represents the amount of matter making up an object, and it is usually measured in **grams (g)** or **kilograms (kg)**. As mass increases, the number of particles increases. For example, if you have two blocks of aluminum with different masses, then the block with the larger mass actually contains more aluminum particles. In fact, if scientists know the chemical composition of the matter, they can calculate a reasonably accurate estimate of the number of particles in the given amount.

Particles of solid ice (molecules made up of two hydrogen atoms and one oxygen atom) are attracted to each other. The force of attraction is strong, which means that the particles don't move around very much. This makes them rigid. Each molecule is able to vibrate a bit, but the strong attraction between the molecules prevents much motion. As a result, a solid block of ice keeps its shape even if we put it inside a beaker, a plastic bag, or a bowl.

Three Phases of Water Molecules

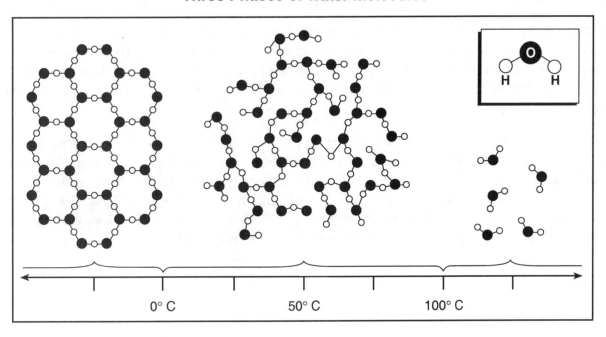

© 2001 Buckle Down Publishing Company. DO NOT DUPLICATE.

As heat is added to the ice, the temperature rises, and the ice melts. The mass of the ice, however, remains the same. Remember that mass is the amount of matter, and that has not changed. The volume will change only slightly. As heat energy is added, the molecules vibrate more and the force of attraction between adjacent molecules is a tiny bit weaker. Notice that in the liquid form, water molecules get closer together than in the solid form. This is a unique property of water: All other compounds spread apart as they melt. We call this *thermal expansion*. You have probably seen examples of thermal expansion. When it gets hot in the summer, sidewalks expand, and the grass or tar between the sidewalks gets squeezed out. If two pieces of sidewalk are too close together, they will collide and possibly crack as they expand. When the sidewalks cool off in the winter, they contract. As the temperature decreases, the particles of matter move closer together. These changes in matter are not very drastic, so you may not be able to measure them easily.

If we add enough heat to a block of ice, it eventually melts, or changes from a solid to a liquid state. In a liquid, the atoms are still attracted to each other, but they have enough energy that they vibrate a great deal and move around easily. If we measured the mass, volume, and temperature of liquid water, we could use a thermometer for temperature and a scale or balance for mass. However, we could not use a ruler to measure volume because liquid water does not have length, width, or height. When we measure liquids, we use a **graduated cylinder**. These are very much like the measuring cups that you might have in your kitchen at home, only more exact. The units on a graduated cylinder are liters (l) or milliliters (ml).

The mass and volume of matter can be compared by using a single term called **density**. Density measures how much matter (mass) is contained in a specific space (volume). As we saw earlier, liquid water is unique in that its molecules are packed closer together than those of solid ice. In other words, water is denser than ice. This is why ice floats in water, and why lakes freeze from the top down.

The density of pure water at 4° C is 1.0 g/cm³ (gram per cubic centimeter) or 1.0 g/ml (gram per milliliter). Even though water expands when it freezes, its mass does not change. Therefore, the density of ice is lower than water, 0.92 g/cm³. Other common substances have the following densities: sea water's density is 1.02 g/cm³; aluminum's density is 2.70 g/cm³; lead's density is 11.3 g/cm³; and cork's density is 0.24 g/cm³. Density is another property of matter that can be used to describe matter and to make predictions about it.

© 2001 Buckle Down Publishing Company. DO NOT DUPLICATE.

In the graduated cylinder below, 50 g of ice were melted. Draw the resulting level of liquid water. State your reasoning for drawing the amount of water you drew.

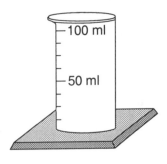

_____

_____

_____

It doesn't matter what container you put a liquid into, you will always have the same amount. The *shape* of the liquid changes, however, as you put it in different containers. This is easily explained by the lowered force of attraction between particles. They are still attracted to each other but not as strongly, so the individual particles can shift around to fill any space instead of being bound up together.

What happens to the shape of water as it is poured from a pitcher to a glass to a bowl? What happens to its volume?

_____

_____

If we continue to add heat to water, the temperature will continue to rise. Eventually, we can boil the water and form gaseous water, or steam. In the gaseous state, there is no attraction between particles. Each individual atom, or molecule, has so much energy that it vibrates and moves independently of the other atoms or molecules. This is why gases take up so much space. The atoms or molecules are moving so quickly and in all directions that they bounce around, occupying all the space available. Gases will still have the same mass because the number of particles is constant. A gas's volume and shape are not fixed. Because each particle is moving independently, the gas will move around to fill its container. For this reason, we say that the volume of a gas is the volume of its container.

© 2001 Buckle Down Publishing Company. DO NOT DUPLICATE.

Using What You Know

Measuring matter is important when doing science. You are going to measure several items in a variety of different ways. Your teacher will give you several items to measure. You will need a metric ruler, a graduated cylinder, water, and access to a scale.

Reminder of some volume formulas:

Box or cube $\qquad V = \text{length} \times \text{width} \times \text{height}$

Cylinder $\qquad V = \text{area of base} \times \text{height} = \pi r^2 \times h$

Sphere $\qquad V = \frac{4}{3} \pi r^3$

Step 1: Calculate the volume of each regularly shaped object by taking direct measurements with your ruler. Hint: Taking measurements of the sphere may require the creative approach of using two books or blocks of wood to determine its diameter. Remember, the radius is half of the diameter. Record your measurements in the following table.

Step 2: Put water into your graduated cylinder, filling it about halfway to the top. Record the water level.

Step 3: Gently slide one of your objects into the graduated cylinder. Record the new volume, then record the volume of the object by subtracting the original volume (Step 2) from the new volume (Step 3).

Step 4: Remove the item and repeat Steps 2 and 3 for all of the other regularly shaped objects.

Step 5: Repeat Steps 2 and 3 for all of the irregularly shaped objects.

	Ruler Measurements		Graduated Cylinder Measurements		
Object	Length, width, height, and radius	Volume	Water level without object (Step 2)	Water level with object (Step 3)	Object volume (Steps 2 and 3)
Cube/block					
Cylinder					
Sphere					
Irregular object					

© 2001 Buckle Down Publishing Company. DO NOT DUPLICATE.

Think It Over

1. Explain why the water level rose from Step 2 to Step 3. What characteristic of matter accounts for this change?

_____

_____

_____

2. How does the calculated volume of the object compare to the change in water level found after you subtracted the original volume from the new volume?

_____

_____

_____

3. When an object placed in water causes the water level to change, this is called *displacement*. We can find the volume of the object by figuring out how much water it displaces.

   Some objects float in water. If we put them into a graduated cylinder of water, only part of the object would be submerged. Why would you need to push the object completely under water to find its volume?

_____

_____

_____

_____

© 2001 Buckle Down Publishing Company. DO NOT DUPLICATE.

Practice Questions

1. Which state of matter allows volume measurements to be made using a ruler?

   A. solid

   B. liquid

   C. gas

   D. plasma

2. Which states of matter have fixed volume and mass?

   A. gas and liquid

   B. gas and solid

   C. liquid and solid

   D. gas, liquid, and solid

3. Which thermometer shows the coldest temperature?

   A. 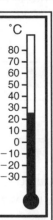   B. 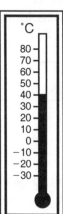   C. 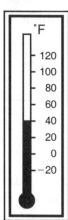   D.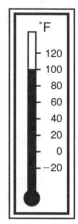

4. What tool is most appropriate for measuring mass?

   A. metric ruler

   B. scale or balance

   C. thermometer

   D. graduated cylinder and water

5. Which statement best describes a liquid?

   A. Shape varies, but volume and mass remain constant.

   B. Mass remains constant, but volume and shape vary by container.

   C. There is no attraction between molecules, allowing free movement of molecules.

   D. The attraction between molecules is very strong, allowing small vibrations only.

6. A cube has a 5 cm edge. What is its volume?

   A. 5 cm^3

   B. 15 cm

   C. 25 cm^2

   D. 125 cm^3

© 2001 Buckle Down Publishing Company. DO NOT DUPLICATE.

Review 12
Physical and Chemical Changes

Have you ever tried to guess what's inside a wrapped package? You look at its size and shape, shake it, squeeze it, and even smell it. In a way, scientists do the same thing in their investigations of matter. They observe and test to see what the properties of matter are so that they can speculate what it is and how it is put together. Much of the information about a type of matter is invisible to the scientist, just as if it were inside a wrapped package. Scientists have used indirect methods of observation to learn a great deal about the structure of matter.

What Do You Think?

As you learned in Review 11, everything in the universe is made up of matter, but not all types of matter have the same properties. You already saw that the same matter in different states, or phases, doesn't even have the same properties.

Imagine that you have a glass of water and a glass of ice. What properties of water and ice make them similar?

_____

_____

_____

What properties of water and ice make them different?

_____

_____

What could you do to make water into ice or ice into water?

_____

_____

Key Words

atom
chemical change
chemical formula
chemical properties
chemical reaction
compound
electron
element
endothermic
exothermic
molecule
neutron
octet rule
outer shell
periodic table of the
   elements
physical properties
proton

© 2001 Buckle Down Publishing Company. DO NOT DUPLICATE.

What People Think

As you know, matter is a general term for the material that makes up everything. Each form of matter has unique properties that help us tell it apart from other types of matter. Some of these properties include color, shape, density, odor, melting and boiling points, hardness, and texture. We can observe such **physical properties** without changing the matter itself.

When heat is added to matter, however, it can change the matter. Remember that in solids, the particles (atoms and molecules) are closely packed together in a tight, orderly, repeating pattern. As heat is added to a solid, the bonds are weakened slightly. That's why most solids will expand, or take up more space, as heat is added.

Matter also has **chemical properties**. Chemical properties are the characteristics of a substance that describe what will happen when it interacts with other substances. If a substance undergoes a **chemical change**, that means that a new substance has been formed. This new substance will no longer have the same chemical properties as the original substance. When you eat lunch, for example, the food you swallow comes into contact with acid in your stomach. The food undergoes a chemical change, and new substances are formed. Some signs of chemical change are color changes, gases being produced, or temperature changes.

During a chemical change, there are interactions among atoms, molecules, or both. **Atoms** are the smallest particles that have the properties of an **element**. An atom has a nucleus in which there are **protons**, which are positively charged, and **neutrons**, which have no charge. Around the nucleus, negatively charged **electrons** travel in specific orbits. The space for each orbit is called a *shell*. Each shell can hold only a certain number of electrons.

Elements combine to form **compounds**. There are thousands and thousands of different compounds. **Molecules** are the smallest particle of a compound having the properties of that compound. Chemical changes occur through an exchange of electrons in the **outer shell** of atoms involved in the change. This exchange of electrons creates a new molecule with its own unique properties. For example, sodium (which has the chemical symbol Na) is a shiny metal that is very reactive in water. Chlorine (chemical symbol Cl) is a poisonous green gas. When sodium and chlorine are combined, an electron from the outer shell of sodium is transferred to the outer shell of chlorine. The result is the formation of a stable, white crystal called sodium chloride: table salt! Its **chemical formula** is NaCl. How do we know that only one sodium atom and one chlorine atom are needed? If we look at the **periodic table of the elements**, found on page 99, the answer becomes clear.

The periodic table arranges the elements in a specific way, based on the structure of their atoms. The column number for a given element corresponds to the number of electrons in the outer shell. You might remember that an atom is most stable when its outer shell is filled. The only elements that naturally have a completely filled outer shell are those in the VIII A column. In order for other atoms to become more stable, they will take electrons, lose electrons, or share electrons so that their outermost shell is filled. This is often referred to as the **octet rule** because it takes eight electrons to fill the outer shell.

© 2001 Buckle Down Publishing Company. DO NOT DUPLICATE.

Periodic Table of the Elements

IA																	VIII A
1 **H** Hydrogen 1.0	II A											III A	IV A	V A	VI A	VII A	2 **He** Helium 4.0
3 **Li** Lithium 6.9	4 **Be** Beryllium 9.0					VIII B						5 **B** Boron 10.8	6 **C** Carbon 12.0	7 **N** Nitrogen 14.0	8 **O** Oxygen 16.0	9 **F** Fluorine 19.0	10 **Ne** Neon 20.2
11 **Na** Sodium 23.0	12 **Mg** Magnesium 24.3	III B	IV B	V B	VI B	VII B	Transition elements		I B	II B		13 **Al** Aluminum 27.0	14 **Si** Silicon 28.1	15 **P** Phosphorus 31.0	16 **S** Sulfur 32.1	17 **Cl** Chlorine 35.5	18 **Ar** Argon 39.9
19 **K** Potassium 39.1	20 **Ca** Calcium 40.1	21 **Sc** Scandium 45.0	22 **Ti** Titanium 47.9	23 **V** Vanadium 51.0	24 **Cr** Chromium 52.0	25 **Mn** Manganese 54.9	26 **Fe** Iron 55.8	27 **Co** Cobalt 58.9	28 **Ni** Nickel 58.7	29 **Cu** Copper 63.5	30 **Zn** Zinc 65.4	31 **Ga** Gallium 69.7	32 **Ge** Germanium 72.6	33 **As** Arsenic 74.9	34 **Se** Selenium 79.0	35 **Br** Bromine 79.9	36 **Kr** Krypton 83.8
37 **Rb** Rubidium 85.5	38 **Sr** Strontium 87.6	39 **Y** Yttrium 88.9	40 **Zr** Zirconium 91.2	41 **Nb** Niobium 92.9	42 **Mo** Molybdenum 96.0	43 **Tc** Technetium 98.9	44 **Ru** Ruthenium 101.1	45 **Rh** Rhodium 102.9	46 **Pd** Palladium 106.4	47 **Ag** Silver 107.9	48 **Cd** Cadmium 112.4	49 **In** Indium 114.8	50 **Sn** Tin 118.7	51 **Sb** Antimony 121.8	52 **Te** Tellurium 127.6	53 **I** Iodine 126.9	54 **Xe** Xenon 131.3
55 **Cs** Cesium 132.9	56 **Ba** Barium 137.4	57 **La** Lanthanum 138.9	72 **Hf** Hafnium 178.5	73 **Ta** Tantalum 181.0	74 **W** Tungsten 183.9	75 **Re** Rhenium 186.2	76 **Os** Osmium 190.2	77 **Ir** Iridium 192.2	78 **Pt** Platinum 195.1	79 **Au** Gold 197.0	80 **Hg** Mercury 200.6	81 **Ti** Thallium 204.4	82 **Pb** Lead 207.2	83 **Bi** Bismuth 209.0	84 **Po** Polonium 209	85 **At** Astatine 210	86 **Rn** Radon 222
87 **Fr** Francium (223)	88 **Ra** Radium (226)	89 **Ac** Actinium (227)	104 **Rf** Rutherfordium (281)	105 **Db** Dubnium (262)	106 **Sg** Seaborgium (263)	107 **Bh** Bohrium (262)	108 **Hs** Hassium (265)	109 **Mt** Meinterium (266)	110 **Uun** UnUnnilium (272)	111 **Uuu** Unununium (272)	112 **UUb** Ununbium (277)						

58 **Ce** Cerium 139	59 **Pr** Praseodymium 141	60 **Nd** Neodymium 144	61 **Pm** Promethium 147	62 **Sm** Samarium 150	63 **Eu** Europium 152	64 **Gd** Gadolinium 157	65 **Tb** Terbium 159	66 **Dy** Dysprosium 162	67 **Ho** Holmium 165	68 **Er** Erbium 167	69 **Tm** Thulium 169	70 **Yb** Ytterbium 173	71 **Lu** Lutetium 175
90 **Th** Thorium (232)	91 **Pa** Protactinium (231)	92 **U** Uranium (238)	93 **Np** Neptunium (237)	94 **Pu** Plutonium (239)	95 **Am** Americium (241)	96 **Cm** Curium (244)	97 **Bk** Berkelium (249)	98 **Cf** Californium (249)	99 **Es** Einsteinium (254)	100 **Fm** Fermium (253)	101 **Md** Mendelevium (256)	102 **No** Nobelium (254)	103 **Lr** Lawrencium (257)

11	— Atomic number
Na	— Symbol
Sodium	— Element
22.990	— Atomic mass

If we follow the octet rule for chlorine, we find that it is an element that has three electron shells (it is found in the third row of the table). There are 17 electrons, seven of which are in the outermost shell (column VII A). For chlorine to have a filled outer shell, it could gain one more electron (thereby having eight in the outermost, third shell) or it could lose seven (thereby having eight in the outermost, second shell).

Sodium is in column I A. This means that it has one electron in its outermost shell. In order for it to satisfy the octet rule, it needs to gain seven electrons or lose one. It's easier to lose one than gain seven, so sodium will give up an electron.

Both atoms can satisfy the octet rule if the sodium gives up an electron and the chlorine accepts that electron. One sodium atom and one chlorine atom are needed to make that happen. Therefore, the compound formed is NaCl.

Why is the chemical formula for water H_2O? Why not HO_2?

_____

_____

All physical and chemical changes involve some type of energy change. Some chemical changes are **exothermic**, meaning that they give off energy as a result of the changes. Burning a piece of charcoal is an example of an exothermic chemical change. Other chemical changes are **endothermic**, which means that a substance absorbs energy. For example, when plants undergo photosynthesis, they absorb light energy.

© 2001 Buckle Down Publishing Company. DO NOT DUPLICATE.

The ice packs that you can find in first-aid kits contain substances that change chemically when you squeeze them together. The packs feel cold when you touch them. Are these packs taking in or giving off heat energy? Explain.

_____

_____

_____

We don't get a compound every time two types of matter come into contact. Sometimes matter forms mixtures. A mixture is a combination of two or more types of matter in which the components retain their individual properties. There is no set ratio for making a mixture. When we make a compound, the elements combine in a set ratio—for example, one oxygen atom for every two hydrogen atoms. In a mixture, that is not the case. If we wanted to make trail mix from peanuts, raisins, and chocolate chips, we could do so no matter how much we have of each ingredient. If you don't have many peanuts, you could make the trail mix with lots of raisins and chocolate chips and only a few peanuts. Likewise, if you only had a few raisins, you could still make trail mix. Mixtures are also easy to separate. You can pick out the raisins by hand because the different kinds of matter are simply sitting near each other. It is not easy to take apart a compound. The atoms are bonded together. It takes a **chemical reaction** to take them apart.

List some examples of mixtures.

_____

_____

When different types of matter interact to form something new, we say that a chemical reaction has taken place. Making trail mix is not a chemical reaction because the peanuts, raisins, and chocolate chips are still the same when we take them out of the mixture. Mixing vinegar and baking soda produces a gas (carbon dioxide) that is clearly different and new. That would be an example of a chemical reaction. Some tell-tale signs of a chemical reaction are changes in temperature or color, bubbling or gas formation, and the creation of new materials that cannot be restored to their original state.

Cooking an egg is a chemical reaction. List some evidence to support that statement.

_____

_____

© 2001 Buckle Down Publishing Company. DO NOT DUPLICATE.

Using What You Know

In this activity, you will have the chance to observe chemical changes taking place. You will need the following materials: a plastic sandwich bag that can be sealed tightly, baking soda, calcium chloride, two plastic spoons, a small beaker that will fit inside the plastic bag (an empty film canister will also work), and safety goggles.

Step 1: Put one level spoonful of baking soda in the plastic bag.

Now use the other spoon to place two level spoonfuls of calcium chloride in the bag. Stir the two substances together and then record your results in the chart that follows Step 2.

Step 2: Fill the small beaker three-quarters full with water. Carefully set the beaker inside the plastic bag on a tabletop without spilling the liquid, as shown in the illustration. Gently squeeze the air out of the bag and seal it. Tip the beaker of water over onto the baking soda and calcium chloride mixture. Record your observations in the chart.

Mixture	Results
Step 1: baking soda, calcium chloride	
Step 2: water, baking soda, calcium chloride	

© 2001 Buckle Down Publishing Company. DO NOT DUPLICATE.

Think It Over

1. Describe the change that took place when you mixed the chemicals together in Step 1. What kind of change was it? Explain your answer.

   _____

   _____

2. Describe the change that took place when you poured the water on the chemicals in Step 2. What kind of change was it? Explain your answer.

   _____

   _____

3. Calcium chloride is a chemical that is often spread on icy sidewalks and roads. What properties of calcium chloride make it useful for melting ice?

   _____

   _____

4. If you could sweep and collect the material left on the sidewalk after you melted the ice with calcium chloride, could you use it again to melt more ice? Explain.

   _____

   _____

5. A large part of the Statue of Liberty is made of copper, yet the outside of the Statue isn't copper-colored at all. Instead, it has a greenish-blue color. Why do you think this is so?

   _____

   _____

© 2001 Buckle Down Publishing Company. DO NOT DUPLICATE.

Practice Questions

1. What happens to a solid (other than ice) as heat is added?

    A. Its density increases.

    B. Its melting point increases.

    C. It begins to take up more space.

    D. The bonds between molecules get tighter.

2. Which of the following is a chemical change?

    A. a nail rusting in the rain

    B. crushing an aspirin tablet into a powder

    C. hammering a piece of metal until it is flat

    D. a swimming pool freezing solid during the winter

3. Judy added a small amount of acid to a beaker containing some water. She noticed that the beaker felt very warm after mixing the two chemicals. Which type of energy change occurred?

    A. exothermic because energy was absorbed

    B. exothermic because energy was released

    C. endothermic because energy was released

    D. endothermic because energy was absorbed

4. Which of these is not a physical property?

    A. phase

    B. density

    C. chemical composition

    D. amount of surface area

5. Which of these is primarily a chemical change?

    A. burning

    B. evaporation

    C. thermal expansion

    D. dissolving in water

© 2001 Buckle Down Publishing Company. DO NOT DUPLICATE.

Directions: Use the following illustration to answer Numbers 6 and 7.

6. Where in the illustration is a chemical change taking place?

   A. in the metal of the bucket, because the candle heats it

   B. in the balloon, because the gas particles are moving faster

   C. in the ice, because the matter is changing from a solid to a liquid

   D. in the candle, because the wick reacts with oxygen during the burning

7. Grace weighed the metal bucket, the ice, and the balloon before lighting the candle. After all the ice melted, the water eventually started to boil. When she weighed the materials later, the mass was less than what she started with. Explain her results.

   _____

   _____

   _____

   _____

© 2001 Buckle Down Publishing Company. DO NOT DUPLICATE.

Review 13
Energy Transformations

Have you ever seen a waterfall and stopped to think about how it could generate the electricity you need to help you finish your homework? Or have you wondered how gasoline can make a car move? Maybe not, but the world around us is full of examples of **energy** and matter being transformed in ways that directly affect our daily lives. After you have completed this review, you will probably notice many more examples of these energy transformations in your life.

What Do You Think?

Our everyday lives are filled with examples of energy being used. Electricity is used to turn on lights, heat your home, and run the vacuum. What we may not think about is that many forms of energy are actually transformed from one type into another. Look at the following illustration.

List at least four examples of energy being used and/or transformed into another type of energy in this illustration.

_____

_____

_____

_____

People frequently say they "used up the electricity in a battery." What actually happens to this energy?

_____

_____

Key Words

chemical energy

conservation of energy

electrical energy

energy

kinetic energy

mechanical energy

nuclear energy

potential energy

radiant energy

solar energy

sound energy

thermal energy

work

© 2001 Buckle Down Publishing Company. DO NOT DUPLICATE.

What People Think

Energy is the ability to make things move or change. When energy is used to create a force that makes something move or change, scientists say **work** has been done. It is very difficult to think of any event happening in our daily lives that doesn't involve energy. However, the law of **conservation of energy** states that energy cannot be created or destroyed. The total amount of energy always stays the same.

There are two basic types of energy that are defined by whether or not an object is moving. **Potential energy**, the first of these, is stored energy. For example, a stone sitting on top of a hill has the "potential" to roll down the hill and do work. The greater that stone's mass, the greater its potential energy. Energy that depends upon height above the Earth's surface is called *gravitational potential energy*. This means that the higher the hill, the more potential energy the stone would have. **Kinetic energy**, the other of these basic types of energy, is energy of motion in an object. Kinetic energy depends on the mass, the speed, and the direction of an object. If the stone were to roll down the hill, its potential energy would be changed into kinetic energy.

Give at least three examples each of potential and kinetic energy.

Potential: _____

_____

_____

Kinetic: _____

_____

_____

Energy exists in various forms besides potential and kinetic energy, and it can be transformed from one type to another. These other types of energy are as follows:

- **Mechanical energy** is the type of energy that moves objects or does work. When an ax strikes a tree, for example, it moves chunks of the wood as it cuts.

- **Thermal energy** is the heat you feel an object give off as a result of the kinetic energy of its moving particles. You feel heat coming off a pot of boiling water because of the fast-moving molecules of water.

- **Electrical energy** is the flow of electrons among atoms in an object that conducts electricity.

- **Nuclear energy** comes from the fission or fusion of the nuclei of atoms. Fission splits atoms, and fusion binds them together. These processes can generate a tremendous amount of energy.

© 2001 Buckle Down Publishing Company. DO NOT DUPLICATE.

- **Radiant energy** is energy that can flow through empty space, such as light, radio waves, or X-rays. Solar energy is an example of radiant energy.

- **Solar energy** is a major source of energy that comes from the Sun. It is a subcategory of radiant energy.

- **Chemical energy** comes from the bonds between atoms in molecules. When a chemical change takes place, chemical energy is given off; one example is gasoline burning in a car engine.

- **Sound energy** comes from the vibration of molecules in the surrounding medium, usually air.

List five examples of energy transformations in your daily life.

_____

_____

_____

_____

_____

Energy that can only be used once is called *nonrenewable energy*. Fossil fuels, which are a major source of energy for the United States, are nonrenewable. Energy that can be used again is called *renewable*. Solar and wind energy are examples of renewable energy.

Give an example of another type of renewable energy and describe how it can be used.

_____

_____

_____

It is important to realize that energy transformations are never 100% efficient. By-products are created, and this makes the energy transformation incomplete. For example, when electrical energy is used to light a bulb in a lamp, not all of the electrical energy turns into light. Some is given off as heat (thermal) energy.

© 2001 Buckle Down Publishing Company. DO NOT DUPLICATE.

Why do you think that the potential energy of a car parked on a hill is not completely changed into kinetic energy when the car rolls down the hill?

_____

_____

_____

_____

_____

Using What You Know

In this activity, you will have the chance to learn more about energy transformations. You will need a piece of cardboard, some construction paper, some tape, books, a meterstick, a toy car, and a flat, even surface.

Step 1: Use a piece of cardboard and some construction paper to build a ramp that is 30 cm long, as shown in the following drawing. The chart that follows Step 2 lists six different heights for the ramp. Use books to change the height of the ramp for each trial of this activity, and use a meterstick to measure the height, not of the books, but of the ramp at its top edge.

© 2001 Buckle Down Publishing Company. DO NOT DUPLICATE.

Step 2: The toy car should start out at the top of the cardboard ramp, its back wheels even with the top edge of the ramp. Make sure you always have the same starting point. One partner should release the car without pushing it, and the other partner should use the meterstick to measure how far the car travels across the room. Measure the distance traveled from the end of the ramp to the car. Record your data each time in the following chart.

Ramp Height	Distance Car Traveled
0 cm (flat)	cm
5 cm	cm
10 cm	cm
15 cm	cm
20 cm	cm
25 cm	cm

Step 3: Make a graph of your data from the chart using the grid provided.

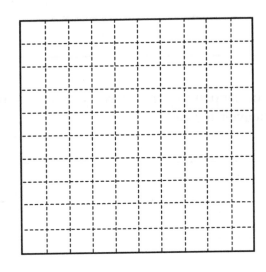

Distance Car Traveled (cm)

Ramp Height (cm)

© 2001 Buckle Down Publishing Company. DO NOT DUPLICATE.

Think It Over

1. What does the graph in Step 3 show you about the changes in the toy car's potential and kinetic energy for each trial?

   _____

   _____

   _____

2. Still using the graph in Step 3, at what point on the ramp is the car's kinetic energy equal to zero? Where is the kinetic energy the greatest?

   _____

   _____

   Where is the potential energy equal to zero? Where is the potential energy the greatest?

   _____

   _____

3. What do you think might happen to your energy graph if the toy car you used were replaced with a much heavier toy car?

   _____

   _____

   _____

4. Below is a list of events. Fill in the blanks to most accurately describe the energy transformations taking place in each. (There might be more than one correct answer in each case.)

   Toasting bread: _____ energy to _____ energy.

   Burning wood: _____ energy to _____ energy.

   Salt melting ice: _____ energy to _____ energy.

© 2001 Buckle Down Publishing Company. DO NOT DUPLICATE.

Practice Questions

Directions: Look at the following illustration, then use it to answer Numbers 1 and 2.

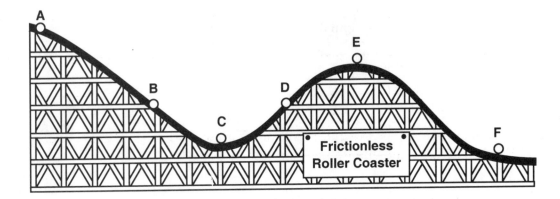

1. Sara and Nicole were discussing the potential energy of the roller coaster cars. Which of the following statements would be the most accurate?

   A. The cars have the least potential energy at position A.

   B. The cars have the most potential energy at position A.

   C. The cars have the least potential energy at position C.

   D. The cars have the most potential energy at position C.

2. As Sara and Nicole travel from position B to position D, what happens to their kinetic energy?

   A. It steadily increases.

   B. It steadily decreases.

   C. It first increases, then decreases.

   D. It first decreases, then increases.

© 2001 Buckle Down Publishing Company. DO NOT DUPLICATE.

Directions: Fred carried out an experiment to test how high a tennis ball would bounce after being dropped from different heights. He used a meterstick held vertically to measure the height from which the ball was dropped and also how high it bounced back up. His results are shown in the following table. Use the information to answer Numbers 3 and 4.

Height Ball Dropped (cm)	Height Ball Bounced (cm)
5	3
25	20
50	39
75	62

3. Which of the following statements about gravitational potential energy (GPE) is true for Fred's experiment?

   A. GPE is the same for all four drop heights.

   B. GPE decreases as the drop height increases.

   C. GPE increases as the drop height decreases.

   D. GPE increases as the drop height increases.

4. If Fred used a Ping-Pong ball instead of the tennis ball in his experiment, which of the following would be true of the gravitational potential energy (GPE)?

   A. The mass of the ball does not influence the GPE.

   B. The GPE of the Ping-Pong ball is less than that of the tennis ball.

   C. The GPE of the Ping-Pong ball is greater than that of the tennis ball.

   D. The GPE of the Ping-Pong ball would be the same as that of the tennis ball.

5. When a candle burns, energy is transformed from

   A. radiant energy to light energy.

   B. thermal energy to mechanical energy.

   C. chemical energy to light and thermal energy.

   D. thermal energy to chemical and radiant energy.

© 2001 Buckle Down Publishing Company. DO NOT DUPLICATE.

Review 14
Electricity and Magnetism

Where does electricity come from? The easy answer is to say, "Out of an outlet in the wall." Are there electrons sitting in the wall, waiting for us to plug something in? Not really. The only thing most people know for sure is that the electricity coming from the outlet is generated somewhere, somehow. But there's more to know about where electricity comes from and why we can depend on it to do all that it does.

What Do You Think?

Electricity is one of the most versatile forces in the world. We use it in dozens of ways every day.

What is electricity?

_____

_____

_____

How does electricity travel so quickly from where it is made, through the wires, and into the appliances in your home?

_____

_____

_____

What People Think

Charged particles in atoms make magnetic fields. Changing magnetic fields cause negatively charged particles, usually electrons, to move. It is this relationship between electric and magnetic fields that allows us to "make" electricity. Electricity-generating plants have huge **turbines** wrapped with thousands of coils of copper wire. These turbines rotate next to strong magnets. Therefore, when the turbines turn, they are moving in a magnetic field. This creates a force on the electrons in the turbine wire, causing those electrons to move.

Key Words

circuit

conductor

electric current

electromagnet

parallel circuit

resistance

series circuit

turbine

© 2001 Buckle Down Publishing Company. DO NOT DUPLICATE.

The moving electrons in a wire are called an **electric current**. Once electricity is produced, it can travel through wires over great distances. When it is in our homes, we are able to use it to make lights and appliances work. The more current that flows through a bulb, the brighter it is.

Electricity won't move through every substance. Glass, plastic, and wood are not good **conductors**, but metals such as copper and aluminum are. Copper wire is used in homes and businesses because it's one of the best conductors. Other forms of metal are not as good. These other conductors, such as steel, have higher **resistance**. The higher the resistance, the more force it takes to push the current through.

If electricity is moving through a lamp, why don't you feel an electrical shock when you turn off the switch?

_____

_____

_____

Anything that works by electricity is part of a **circuit**. In your home, an electrical circuit has a source of energy, wires to carry it, a switch to turn it on and off, and something to be operated by electricity. Many electric devices have complicated patterns of circuitry, yet there are only two basic types of circuits: series and parallel.

In a **series circuit**, the current goes along a single path through every part of the circuit. If the current is interrupted anywhere, the circuit will not work. A string of Christmas lights can be wired in series. If one bulb burns out, none of the bulbs will light.

In a **parallel circuit**, there is more than one path for the current to travel. If one path is interrupted, the current can take another, and the circuit will still operate. The electricity in your house is wired in parallel. In your kitchen, for example, the refrigerator will work even if the toaster shuts off. If the kitchen were wired in series, all the appliances would have to be on for any one of them to work. But because the kitchen is wired in parallel, there are multiple paths for the electric current to take.

For everything in a circuit to work properly, the current must be strong enough to operate the device connected to the circuit. The current also must have enough force to move through the circuit. If the current lacks strength or force, the device may not work properly. For example, a light bulb connected to the circuit may fail to light or may not burn brightly.

© 2001 Buckle Down Publishing Company. DO NOT DUPLICATE.

Describe the difference between a series circuit and a parallel circuit.

_____

_____

_____

_____

What limits the ability of electric current to move through a conductor? Why is this a useful thing to be able to control?

_____

_____

_____

_____

You know that some magnets occur in nature. Others are made by humans. There are three main ways to make a magnet: You can rub a metal object with a magnet; you can cool a heated piece of iron near a strong magnet; or you can make an **electromagnet**. Just as magnets can be used to create electricity, electricity can be used to create magnets. Electromagnets are made by running electric current through wire that is wrapped around a metal object. The electric current in the wire has a magnetic field that causes the magnetic fields of the metal's atoms to line up. When the electric current is turned off, the metal is no longer magnetic. A simple example of an electromagnet is a loop of wire wrapped around a nail.

Why are electromagnets rather than natural magnets used to pick up scrap metal in junkyards?

_____

_____

_____

© 2001 Buckle Down Publishing Company. DO NOT DUPLICATE.

Using What You Know

Your teacher will give you some batteries, lightbulbs, and wires.

Step 1: Study the four circuits shown. For each circuit, predict whether the bulb will light and, if so, how brightly it will burn. Write your predictions in the second and third columns of the table that follows the circuit diagrams.

Step 2: Test your predictions by building each of the four circuits. Note the results of your experiments in the table and compare them to your predictions.

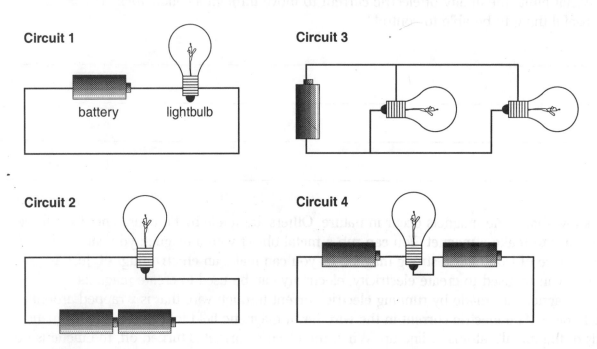

Circuit	Will it light? (Prediction)	How bright will it be?	Did it light? (Result)	How bright was it?
1				
2				
3				
4				

© 2001 Buckle Down Publishing Company. DO NOT DUPLICATE.

Think It Over

1. Which bulb will be brighter: one bulb with one battery, or one bulb with two batteries wired in series? Give reasons for your answer.

_____

_____

_____

2. Which will be brighter: one bulb with one battery or two bulbs with one battery wired in series? Give reasons for your answer.

_____

_____

_____

Practice Questions

1. You walk into the living room and turn on a light switch. Usually, three lights come on. This time, however, only two come on. How is the circuit containing the lights wired?

   A. open

   B. series

   C. parallel

   D. More information is needed to answer the question.

2. You have a series circuit with two bulbs in it. What would happen if you turned the battery around?

   A. Both bulbs would go out.

   B. Both lights would remain lit.

   C. The bulb closest to the battery would go out.

   D. The bulb farthest from the battery would go out.

© 2001 Buckle Down Publishing Company. DO NOT DUPLICATE.

Directions: A circuit is made as shown here. The three bulbs are all the same. Study the diagram, then answer Numbers 3 and 4.

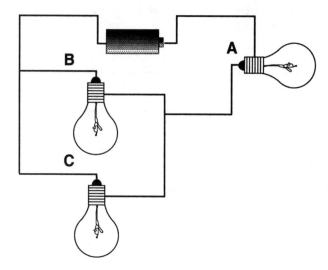

3. Which bulb will burn brightest?
   A. bulb A
   B. bulb B
   C. bulb C
   D. All three bulbs will burn equally as bright.

4. Where could you place a switch that would operate all three bulbs?
   A. just to the left of bulb C
   B. just to the right of bulb B
   C. just to the right of bulb C
   D. between bulb A and the battery

5. High-speed trains are being researched that utilize magnetic fields to levitate the train above the tracks. This drastically reduces the friction on the train's wheels, allowing it to reach speeds upwards of 300 miles per hour! Using what you know about magnetic fields, gravity, and electricity, explain how such a train might work.

_____

_____

_____

_____

_____

© 2001 Buckle Down Publishing Company. DO NOT DUPLICATE.

Review 15
Chemical Pollution

Natural forces have been shaping the Earth's surface throughout its existence. Sometimes these natural changes damage ecosystems. For example, natural events such as volcanic eruptions create an enormous amount of **pollution**, which drastically affects the climate and ecosystems around the volcano. Most of what we call *pollution*, however, stems from human activity. In this review, you will learn about the impact that humans have on the quality of the air, water, and land that support life on Earth.

What Do You Think?

Pollution has been a problem for humans as long as we have formed societies. Until about 200 years ago, only large cities had major pollution problems. However, as our population has increased and industrial technology has expanded, virtually no place on Earth could now be described as safe from human pollution.

List three forms of pollution that have been with us since the beginning of human society.

_____

_____

_____

List three forms of pollution that have become a problem in the last 200 years.

_____

_____

_____

What People Think

Until the second half of the 20th century, humans had virtually no restrictions on the pollution that factories and individuals could release into the air. Over time, conditions grew worse and worse, leading to some frightening episodes. For instance, in the 1950s, a polluted fog in London killed thousands of people in just five days. Soon people began to question all the effects that air pollution might have in their own cities and towns. Federal, state, and local governments made laws that regulated the type and amount of pollution an industry could

Key Words

aquifer

greenhouse effect

groundwater

hydrocarbon

pollution

smog

thermal pollution

watershed

© 2001 Buckle Down Publishing Company. DO NOT DUPLICATE.

release. Homes started to burn cleaner oil and natural gas instead of smoky coal. Scientists carried out extensive research to detemine ways to make cars run on cleaner fuel.

Even though many improvements have been put in place, air pollution still remains a threat to our environment. Automobile engines are responsible for most air pollution. This may come as a surprise; when someone mentions air pollution, we often think of factory smokestacks pouring smoke into the air. Industy does contribute significantly to air pollution. However, there are millions upon millions of cars on the road every day, and the combined effect of their exhaust causes most air pollution. An automobile engine requires a chemical reaction to create the force needed to move. This reaction involves the burning of **hydrocarbons** from fossil fuels. Gases are released into the atmosphere that are harmful to human health, including sulfur, carbon, and nitrogen compounds. As you learned in Review 2, these gases contribute to the **greenhouse effect**, which is trapping heat within the Earth's atmosphere. Also, many American cities report problems with **smog**, a dangerous fog that results from a reaction between automobile emissions and sunlight. Asthma rates have soared in recent years, especially in urban areas, and many scientists link this epidemic to air pollution.

Improvements have been made. Lead, a major solid pollutant in car exhaust, was removed from gasoline in the 1980s. Automobile manufacturers are researching ways to make cars that burn far less gasoline than current cars. They are aiming to make cars that travel more than 80 miles per gallon, more than double the efficiency of the average car in 2001.

List three ways that you and the people you know could help reduce the amount of pollution released into the air.

_____

_____

_____

_____

_____

The oceans often seem infinitely large to people, so it's no surprise that people once thought that dumping waste into the ocean wouldn't have any harmful effects. However, the world population has increased dramatically in the last century, and the oceans have shown signs that they are unable to absorb any more pollutants. As a result of a lot of hard work and tough negotiations, many nations signed on to the 1972 United Nations Law of the Seas, which (among other things) limits and regulates the pollution released into the oceans. This was a good step, but much work is still needed. As of 1998, more than 50 nations that have seafront or oceanfront land had not yet agreed to the treaty, and the oceans will continue to circulate their pollution around to everyone's shores.

© 2001 Buckle Down Publishing Company. DO NOT DUPLICATE.

Closer to home, many pollution issues endanger our local sources of freshwater. Although the Earth's surface is mostly water, the chart below shows that less than 3% of the total amount of water on Earth is freshwater.

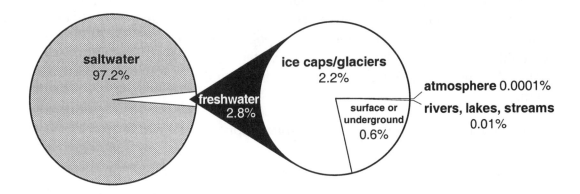

Looking at the amount of freshwater on Earth in the chart above, how much of that is readily available for human use?

_____

Because the amount of freshwater is so limited, we must recycle the water available to us. Scientists divide the land we live in into separate **watersheds**, areas of land that drain into a particular system of creeks, streams, and rivers. From the moment water surfaces at the spring of a watershed to the time it drains into a lake or an ocean, it may be recycled 10 or more times. This means that everyone living in a particular watershed should be concerned with what pollutants are escaping into the water supply.

Using the library and the Internet, identify the watershed that supplies your town or city.

_____

There are a variety of pollutants that can threaten our water supplies. Soil and plant material can erode from farms and pollute the watershed. Sediment from construction projects can clog the waterways, reducing the oxygen necessary to maintain a healthy watershed. Organic waste, or sewage, from humans and farm animals can also pollute water and lead to the growth of poisonous bacteria. Pesticides and fertilizers from farms often seep into the watershed, either killing necessary organisms in the water or causing a dangerous overgrowth of them. **Thermal pollution** occurs when water that is 10° C higher than the natural temperature enters the watershed. This water gets heated by households, factories, reactors, and power plants and can disrupt local ecosystems when it is put back into the watershed. Most dangerously, toxic chemicals can escape from industries along the watershed and threaten the whole region.

© 2001 Buckle Down Publishing Company. DO NOT DUPLICATE.

Pollution can enter the watershed without being put directly into a stream. A significant supply of water called **groundwater** is found in large, underground reservoirs, or **aquifers**. Groundwater can be polluted in many ways. Waste dumps, toxic chemicals, fertilizers, and other hazardous materials commonly cause groundwater pollution. After the chemical is applied or put into the ground, some of it can seep underground through the soil and the layers of rock, ultimately entering the aquifer. Once these pollutants contaminate the groundwater, it becomes very difficult to restore the quality of the water. Groundwater pollution affects the drinking water of many communities, and it can often make the water supply hazardous to human health.

List three possible threats to the watershed that supplies your town or city.

_____

_____

_____

Because the water in a particular watershed can be threatened by such a variety of pollutants, cities and towns invest a lot of time and money in water treatment facilities. These facilities are expensive to maintain and upgrade, so many industries have realized that it is better to concentrate on preventing waste from entering the watershed in the first place.

In addition to air and water pollution, solid-waste pollution poses many problems. Again, the biggest contributor to the solid waste problem isn't big corporations; rather, it is the average family household and the trash and garbage we generate. In many large urban centers, communities are facing a crisis: Landfills made to hold local waste material are reaching maximum capacity. For example, the Fresh Kills Landfill in Staten Island, New York, is currently scheduled to close within the next few years because there is no longer any room to bury all the garbage produced in the metropolitan area. Yet this site is the last remaining landfill in New York City. As a result, many plans have been proposed to ship all waste materials to sites in other states that have the room to bury New York's garbage.

What are the advantages and disadvantages for the people in communities where plans for accepting New York's garbage have been proposed?

_____

_____

_____

© 2001 Buckle Down Publishing Company. DO NOT DUPLICATE.

What are some alternatives to the "ship-and-bury" approach to waste management for New York City?

_____

_____

_____

What are some of the advantages and disadvantages with your answer?

_____

_____

_____

Using What You Know

Where does the water in your area come from? What are some of the pollutants that must be taken out of the water? How is the water delivered to homes?

Look at the questions in the "Think It Over" section, and then organize and conduct an interview with a representative from your local water utility, a sewer treatment facility, or an environmental group. You can run the interview over the phone, in person, or with a written letter. **Important:** Use the questions in the next section as a starting point, but don't use them word-for-word. They won't work as an interview.

Whether you write a letter, make a phone call, or conduct a face-to-face interview, be sure to identify yourself and your school at the first opportunity, state your purpose, and be polite. Find out who in the organization is responsible for public inquiries. When you have gotten answers to your questionnaire, record the name and organization of the person to whom you spoke.

Name: _____

Organization: _____

© 2001 Buckle Down Publishing Company. DO NOT DUPLICATE.

Think It Over

Directions: After you have conducted the interview, use the information you have gathered to answer the questions below.

1. Where does the water for your area come from? Is this a groundwater source or a surface water source?

   _____

   _____

2. What are some typical pollutants that must be removed from the water? Which of these is the greatest threat?

   _____

   _____

   _____

   _____

3. What are some things that could be done to help solve this problem?

   _____

   _____

4. How much water per year does your local utility provide?

   _____

5. Briefly describe the process of water purification in your area.

   _____

   _____

   _____

   _____

© 2001 Buckle Down Publishing Company. DO NOT DUPLICATE.

Practice Questions

1. Many scientists believe that carbon dioxide emissions gather high above the Earth's surface and trap heat in the atmosphere. Also, data show that the burning of fossil fuels has increased the amount of carbon dioxide in the atmosphere by about 10% over the last 30 years. If this trend continues, which of the following would be most likely to occur?

   A. The atmosphere will start to get thinner.

   B. Carbon dioxide concentrations will decrease by 10%.

   C. Temperatures will rise as carbon dioxide concentration increases.

   D. Ozone concentrations will counteract the increase in temperature.

2. A scientist looking at the data from the previous question wants to begin an experiment to test the link between pollution and global warming. Which of the following is a logical first step in testing his hypothesis?

   A. Collect climate data for the past 500 years.

   B. Find out how much carbon dioxide is produced on Earth.

   C. Describe the mechanism by which carbon dioxide absorbs heat.

   D. Determine how temperature fluctuations were caused in the past.

3. Residents of a town detect high levels of a toxic chemical in their wells. The town is located 10 miles from a factory that produces that same chemical. What is the most likely explanation for the pollution in the water supply?

   A. A polluted stream ran from the factory toward the town.

   B. Trucks carrying shipments of the chemical spilled near the town.

   C. A chemical mist was carried from the factory by winds blowing toward the town.

   D. Chemicals from the factory soaked into the soil and reached the local aquifer.

4. Which of the following would not be a practical solution to the problem of fossil fuel emissions?

   A. Form carpools to travel to and from school.

   B. Reduce the hours of service of public buses.

   C. Encourage research in more fuel-efficient automobiles.

   D. Plant many more trees along city streets to absorb carbon dioxide.

© 2001 Buckle Down Publishing Company. DO NOT DUPLICATE.

5. Imagine that you are a member of your local city council. A large, international corporation has said that it wants to open a factory in your town that will employ thousands of people. However, the corporation has been known to break environmental laws in the past. Describe some of the safeguards that you and the city council will enact before allowing the corporation to build the factory.

_____

_____

_____

_____

_____

_____

_____

PEOPLE IN SCIENCE

Rachel Carson
(United States 1907–1964)

Rachel Carson gave up writing so she could study science. Her teachers warned her that science was a man's world and that she should continue to write. Carson believed, however, that she had important work to do as a scientist. She went to college and studied the sea and sea life. Then she got a job at the U. S. Bureau of Fisheries. Her first task was to write about ocean life—her love of nature had led her full circle. From that time on, she used both her knowledge of science and her skills as a writer. In 1958, she took on a new challenge. She wrote about the effects of poisonous insect spray on the environment. She wondered what happened to the pesticide after it was sprayed onto our fields and forests. Did it disappear harmlessly, or, over time, did it kill organisms other than insects? Her book, *Silent Spring*, was the world's first warning about the deadly effects of chemical pesticides on the environment. When it was published in 1962, tens of thousands of people read her book, and President Kennedy ordered further study of pesticides. Thanks to Carson's efforts, we now have laws to protect our environment from dangerous chemicals.

© 2001 Buckle Down Publishing Company. DO NOT DUPLICATE.

Review 16
Force, Inertia, and Acceleration

Have you ever seen a magician pull a tablecloth out from underneath the glasses, plates, and silverware on a table? What's the trick? Does it matter if you pull fast or slow or at an angle? What are the **forces** involved that allow the tablecloth to be pulled off the table without spilling everything on it? In this review, you will see that there is a simple physical law that helps explain this magic trick.

What Do You Think?

When you sit still in a chair, your body's position in relation to the Earth is not changing. But are there any forces acting on you when you are sitting still in the chair?

In the space provided, draw all the forces that are acting on you as you sit in a chair.

Describe the types of forces you have included and how strong they are in relation to each other.

_____

_____

_____

_____

_____

Key Words

force

friction

fulcrum

gravity

inertia

lever

Newton's first law

normal force

simple machine

© 2001 Buckle Down Publishing Company. DO NOT DUPLICATE.

What People Think

For a long time, people believed that objects had a tendency to be at rest. They felt that if something were moving, it would eventually stop moving in order to be in its "natural" state of rest. Scientist Isaac Newton determined that this was not the case. **Newton's first law** (the law of **inertia**) says that if the forces acting on an object are balanced (equal and opposite), the object will continue doing what it is doing. This means that an object at rest will stay at rest, just as people traditionally believed. However, it also means that an object moving at a constant speed in a straight line will keep moving in the same straight line unless acted on by an outside force. This tendency for objects to keep doing what they are doing is caused by inertia. Newton's work in inertia caused the laws of physics to be rewritten.

Give one example of a situation in which you experience inertia.

(1) Turning a car on an icy road

(2) Stopping your bike quickly & completely if moving fast.

The fact that we cannot see a force does not mean it is not there. Invisible forces that typically act on objects include **gravity**, **friction**, and **normal force**. Gravity pulls objects toward the Earth, friction slows down objects, and normal force pushes up to support the weight of an object. If you roll a ball across the room, it has all these forces acting on it. The push you give the ball acts on the ball only while your hand is actually making contact with the ball. Once the ball leaves your hand, you are no longer exerting a force on the ball.

If the law of inertia is true, it seems that the ball you have pushed should continue rolling forever. You know this doesn't happen, however. Why does the ball stop?

The ball stops because friction is acting on it which cause it to stop. Friction is an unbalanced force

Once an object is in motion, we have various ways of describing that motion: direction, speed, velocity, and so on. You've certainly heard speed described in terms of *miles per hour*. In science, terms like *meters per second* are often used. In all cases, speed is measured as distance divided by time. So if a car travels 50 miles in 1 hour, we can say that its speed is 50 miles per hour.

What is the speed of a missile that travels 200 meters in 5 seconds?

$$Speed = \frac{distance}{time} = \frac{200\ meters}{5} = 40\ m/s$$

© 2001 Buckle Down Publishing Company. DO NOT DUPLICATE.

Imagine that you are sitting in a chair. Now imagine that a classmate wants to put a rug down on the floor in the area where you are sitting, but you do not want to move. Of course, it would be difficult for your classmate to pick you and your chair up in order to put the rug down beneath you. If your classmate had a **simple machine**, however, she would be able to move you much more easily.

What kind of simple machine would help your classmate move you?

A lever or a pulley system.

Simple machines might not be what you usually think of as machines. They are not electrical, and they do not have engines. Usually, a person supplies all the force that is needed. Machines help us do work. The scientific definition of *work* is the amount of force needed to move something a certain distance.

If your classmate tries to move you out of your chair, a **lever** would be one kind of simple machine to use. A seesaw is one type of lever; it is a rigid board, or body, that rotates on a point called a **fulcrum**. On a seesaw, if you were to sit close to the fulcrum and try to move a heavier person on the opposite end of the board, it would be difficult to move the other person. You might be able to lift the other person a small distance from the ground, but it would require a lot of force. If you were to move back to the very end of your side of the board, however, it would be much easier for you to lift the other person. In this case, you could lift the person a greater distance off the ground using much less force.

Use the space provided to draw a lever arrangement that would make it easier for your classmate to lift you and your chair completely off the floor.

© 2001 Buckle Down Publishing Company. DO NOT DUPLICATE.

What are some other forms of the lever that you see in everyday life?

_____

_____

Levers are the simplest machines. Other simple machines include the pulley, the wheel and axle, the screw, the wedge, and the inclined plane.

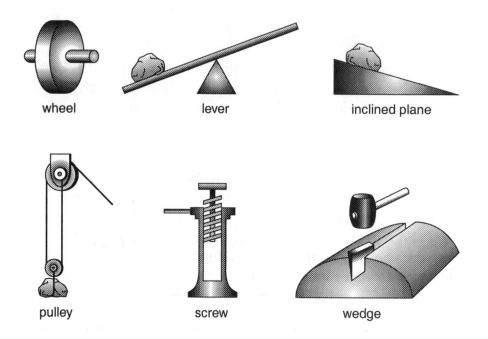

wheel   lever   inclined plane

pulley   screw   wedge

Using What You Know

Your teacher will give you some materials to use in testing ideas about pendulums. You will need a stopwatch for all steps. For Steps 1 through 4, you will also need a ruler and five metal washers attached to varying lengths of string. For Steps 5 through 7, you will need one, three, and five metal washers attached to the same length of string to act as pendulum bobs.

Step 1: In the first part of the activity, you will be determining how the length of a pendulum affects the number of swings the pendulum makes in 10 seconds. Before you begin, predict how you think the number of swings a pendulum makes in 10 seconds will vary as the length of string varies.

_____

_____

_____

© 2001 Buckle Down Publishing Company. DO NOT DUPLICATE.

Step 2: Determine how many swings each of your pendulums makes in 10 seconds. One swing is a complete cycle of the pendulum swinging away from and back to the starting point.

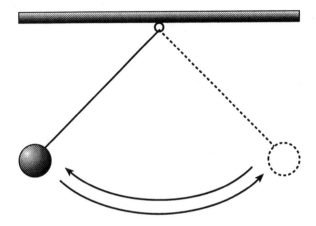

Record your results in the following table:

Step 2

Pendulum	Number of Swings	Length of String
1		
2		
3		
4		
5		

Step 3: Determine the length of each pendulum by measuring each string and bob. Record this information in the table.

© 2001 Buckle Down Publishing Company. DO NOT DUPLICATE.

Step 4: In the grid below, graph your results for how many swings each pendulum makes in 10 seconds. Describe the pattern that is formed. Was your prediction in Step 1 correct, or do you need to modify your original thoughts? Record how you would modify your prediction based on your results.

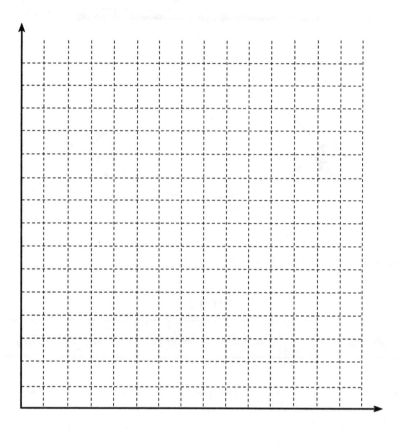

© 2001 Buckle Down Publishing Company. DO NOT DUPLICATE.

Step 5: In this part of the activity, you will determine how the mass of the pendulum washers affects the number of swings a pendulum makes in 10 seconds. You will use three different masses of pendulums: a one-washer pendulum, a three-washer pendulum, and a five-washer pendulum. Before you begin, record your prediction about how you think the mass of each pendulum affects the number of swings made in 10 seconds.

Mass has no effect on the period of the swings.

Step 6: Determine the number of swings each pendulum makes in 10 seconds. Record your results in the following table.

Step 6

Number of Washers	Number of Swings
1	
3	
5	

© 2001 Buckle Down Publishing Company. DO NOT DUPLICATE.

Step 7: Graph your results and summarize how the mass of the pendulum affects the number of swings a pendulum makes in 10 seconds. What modifications do you have to make to your prediction in Step 5 based on your results? Rewrite your prediction based on your results.

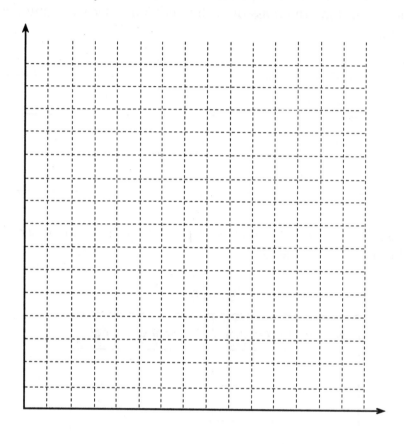

_____

_____

_____

_____

_____

© 2001 Buckle Down Publishing Company. DO NOT DUPLICATE.

Think It Over

1. How does length affect the number of swings a pendulum makes in 10 seconds?

_____

_____

2. How does the mass of the pendulum affect the number of swings a pendulum makes in 10 seconds?

_____

_____

3. What force is acting on the pendulum to make it move downward at the start of each swing?

_____ gravity _____

4. What force is slowing the pendulum down at the end of each swing?

_____ gravity _____

5. At what position during the swing is gravity not causing a change in the motion of the pendulum?

When it is @ the midpoint of the swing. Pendulum is ⊥ to the ground. All gravitational force is counterbalanced by the tension of the swing.

6. Imagine you are in an antique store and there is an old grandfather clock in the corner. A grandfather clock has a pendulum that can keep the time by swinging back and forth every second. The owner of the store complains that the clock "runs too fast." In other words, the pendulum is moving too quickly. How could you modify the clock to make it keep the time correctly?

Lengthen the pendulum.

_____

_____

_____

© 2001 Buckle Down Publishing Company. DO NOT DUPLICATE.

Practice Questions

1. Imagine that an object is moving in a straight line and at a constant speed. Which of the following statements about that object must be true?

   A. There are no forces acting on the object.

   B. The forces acting on the object are balanced.

   C. There is only one force acting on the object.

   D. Only gravity is acting on the object because gravity is always present.

2. Which of the following statements best expresses Newton's first law?

   A. Objects in motion will always slow down and stop.

   B. Objects that have outside forces acting on them will move in a straight line.

   C. Objects at rest will stay at rest unless the forces acting on them change.

   D. Objects in motion will stay in motion no matter how many forces are acting on them.

3. Imagine that a car is being driven with cruise control on, so it is going at a constant speed. Which diagram correctly identifies the forces acting on the car?

   A.
   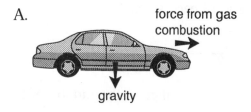
   force from gas combustion
   gravity

   C.

   force from gas combustion

   B.
   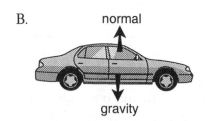
   normal
   gravity

   D.
   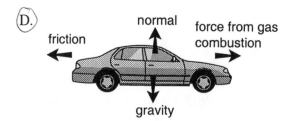
   normal
   friction
   force from gas combustion
   gravity

   all forces are equal & opposite

© 2001 Buckle Down Publishing Company. DO NOT DUPLICATE.

4. A very small child sits on a seesaw at one end. Where should a larger child sit in order for the two to be balanced?

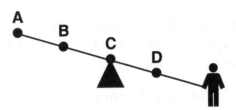

A. A

B. B

C. C

D. D

5. A student pushes against a wall with a force, but the wall does not move. In this situation, the wall exerts

A. no force.

B. less force than the student.

C. the same amount of force as the student.

D. more force than the student.

6. Make a diagram that uses a simple machine to lift a 100 kg box up to a table that is 1.0 m above the ground.

© 2001 Buckle Down Publishing Company. DO NOT DUPLICATE.

Review 17
Sound and Light

If a tree falls in the forest and no one is there to hear it, does it make a sound? Can there be a sound if nobody hears it? These questions lead to others that are somewhat easier to answer: What is sound? How is it that we hear things?

Now, what about light? Consider all of the different ways we use light. Bright white light can be concentrated into a spotlight for a stage. Stoplights on the street regulate traffic. Laser beams of light read the information stored on compact discs and create music. Light shines through moving, colored film to show movies in theaters. What is light? Does it travel like sound?

The key to understanding the interesting similarities and differences between sound and light is to understand the behavior of waves. Both sound and light travel as waves, and both behave like waves. However, as you know, sound and light aren't the same thing. Find out more in this review.

What Do You Think?

A rainbow is a beautiful sight. White sunlight is shining, yet we see different colors.

Where do the different colors of a rainbow come from? In the box provided, draw a diagram showing how a rainbow forms.

Key Words

absorb

echo

lens

longitudinal wave

medium

opaque

optic nerve

pupil

reflection

refraction

retina

scatter

translucent

transparent

transverse wave

vacuum

vibration

wave

© 2001 Buckle Down Publishing Company. DO NOT DUPLICATE.

Explain in words how you think a rainbow is formed.

_____

_____

_____

_____

_____

Now imagine you are standing on one side of a large canyon. Your friend is on the other side. When you call across to her, your voice repeats back to you a few seconds later as an **echo**.

Knowing that sound and light are both **waves**, draw an illustration of how your voice carries across the canyon and comes back to your ears.

Now explain in words how you think an echo works.

_____

_____

_____

© 2001 Buckle Down Publishing Company. DO NOT DUPLICATE.

What People Think

Sound and light both travel as waves, but they are different kinds of waves. Sound is a type of **longitudinal wave**. A spring that rests on a flat surface and is compressed and stretched is an example of a longitudinal wave. The particles that are vibrating do so in the same direction as the wave's motion.

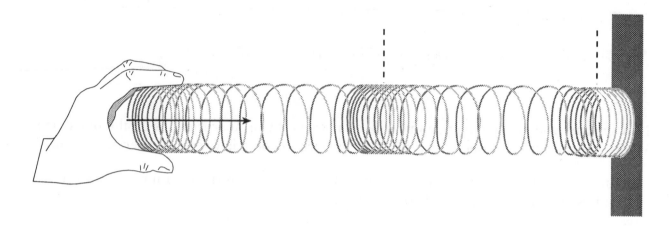

The particles in a **transverse wave**, on the other hand, vibrate in a direction that is perpendicular to the direction in which the wave travels. Light is an example of a transverse wave. The waves that are made by throwing a stone in a pond are an example of transverse waves. The waves travel outward from where the stone land, but the water molecules vibrate up and down. You can also make transverse waves with a spring, as shown in the illustration.

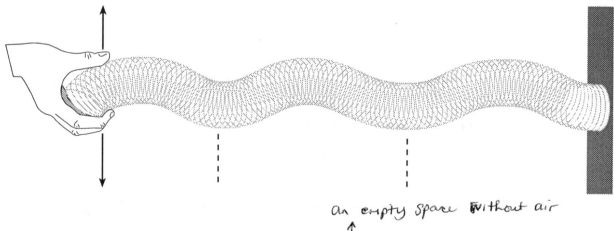

an empty space without air
↑

Transverse waves such as light can travel through a **vacuum**. When light travels through anything else—gases, liquids, or solids—it slows down. Still, when light travels through air, it travels 10,000,000 times faster than sound! For an example of this huge difference in speed, pay attention the next time a thunderstorm rolls through. Lightning and thunder happen at the same instant, yet we often see the lightning before we hear the thunder.

© 2001 Buckle Down Publishing Company. DO NOT DUPLICATE.

In contrast, sound and other longitudinal waves <u>cannot</u> travel through a vacuum. Longitudinal waves require a substance, or **medium**, through which to travel. This is why they cannot travel in a vacuum, which has no molecules to vibrate back and forth. Sound can travel through solids (think about someone upstairs from you dropping a book), liquids (dolphins can communicate with high-pitched squeals), and gases (our voices travel through the air as sound waves). <u>Sound waves travel fastest through a solid, because its molecules are tightly packed:</u> The vibrations don't have to move as far to complete a vibration. <u>Sound waves move more slowly in a liquid and slowest of all in a gas.</u>

Special effects in some movies portray loud, bright explosions in outer space. Explain what is accurate and inaccurate about these special effects.

_____

_____

_____

Sound comes out of our mouths when we speak. But as you know, sound cannot travel through a vacuum. What kind of instruments and materials do we use to create sound? When we speak, our vocal chords vibrate. You can feel these **vibrations** if you touch your throat while speaking. These vibrations are transferred to the molecules in the air, causing them to vibrate. These vibrating air molecules bombard the listener's eardrums, causing them to vibrate as well. The vibrations in the eardrum are transferred through vibrating cilia in the ear and up to the brain where they are processed as sound.

If a room really were empty—in other words, if it didn't have any air in it—the sound would die. There must be something to vibrate in order for sound to travel.

How can you tell whether sound travels through solids or liquids?

_____

_____

If you stand next to someone while they are speaking to you, there is no "time delay" between seeing their lips move and hearing the sound. Why?

_____

_____

© 2001 Buckle Down Publishing Company. DO NOT DUPLICATE.

Light waves have an amplitude, a frequency, and a period. When a light wave's frequency changes, its color changes. Colored objects **absorb** (soak up, like a sponge) all colors except the color that we see. For example, a red book looks red in the sunlight because it absorbs all the colors of the sunlight *except* red. Red light bounces into our eyes, and we see the book as being red. This process is called **reflection**. If only blue light were to shine on that same book, the book would appear to be black! The book absorbs everything but red, so the blue would be absorbed, and there would be nothing to be reflected back. The book would appear black because black is the absence of all color.

Why should clothing stores provide well-lit display areas?

_____

_____

_____

How does our eye translate all these light waves into images and colors? Our eyes function much in the same way as a telescope or a movie camera: The light enters through the **pupil,** which directs it toward the **lens.** The lens then focuses the light and projects it onto the **retina** at the back of the eyeball. There, the **optic nerve** translates the information and delivers it to our brain.

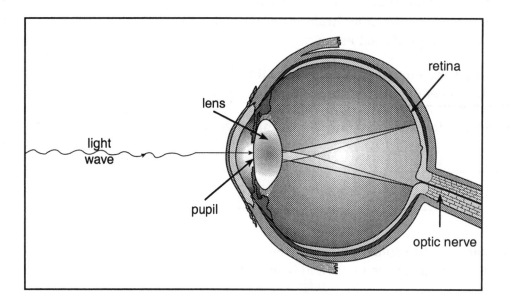

© 2001 Buckle Down Publishing Company. DO NOT DUPLICATE.

Both sound and light waves reflect off things in a predictable way. The incoming angle and the outgoing angle are equal to each other. If the surface a light wave is hitting is highly polished, like a mirror, the reflected light is in a beam. If the surface is not polished, like most surfaces, the reflected light is irregular, going off in all direction; the light is then described as **scattered**. Scattered light still bounces off so that the angles in and out are equal, but the surface it is bouncing off has many different angles.

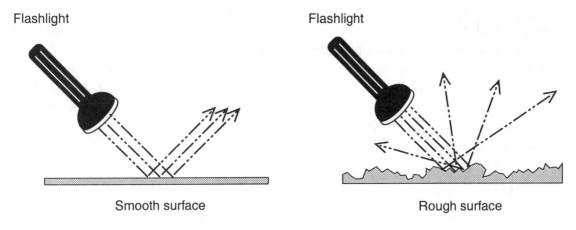

Flashlight   Flashlight

Smooth surface   Rough surface

Think about how an echo occurs. How do sound waves behave when they are scattered?

_____

_____

_____

You know that light is able to pass through some objects, such as windows. A **transparent** object allows most of the light that hits it to pass through, and it absorbs or reflects only a very small amount. A **translucent** object allows only some of the light that hits it to pass through and absorbs or reflects some of it. An object that absorbs or reflects all light that hits it is called **opaque**. Any time light is absorbed, a shadow is produced.

Does a window cast a shadow? Explain.

_____

_____

When light passes through an object, it slows down. Remember that light is a vibration. It is easy for the light to vibrate in air or a vacuum. In a substance that is denser, such as water or glass, the molecules of the substance slow down light's vibrations. This causes the light to slow down. When light changes speed, it bends, or changes direction. This change in direction is called **refraction**.

© 2001 Buckle Down Publishing Company. DO NOT DUPLICATE.

Using What You Know

Your teacher will give you and your partner a flashlight, colored paper, white paper, tape, six different colored crayons, and at least three colored filters.

Part 1

Step 1: You will need to work at a desk, table, or counter that is against a wall. Tape a piece of plain white paper to the wall a few centimeters above your work surface. Set a piece of colored paper flat on your work surface, out of your partner's sight line. Your partner should be standing several feet away from your work surface and should not see what color paper you are using. Shine the flashlight onto the colored paper so that the reflection from it hits the white paper. The following diagram shows you how to set up this activity. Have your partner look at the white paper and decide what color the hidden colored paper is.

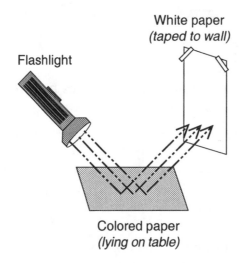

Step 2: Repeat Step 1, trading roles with your partner and trying several different colors of paper.

Part 2

Step 3: On white paper, draw a line with each of the six colors of crayon.

Step 4: Hold one of the colored filters your teacher gives you in front of your eyes and look at the colored lines. Record your observations of how each colored line looks in the table that follows Step 5.

CAUTION: Be sure to hold the filter in front of your eyes like sunglasses. In order to avoid scratching your eyes, do not hold the filters too close to your eyes.

Step 5: Repeat Step 4 with the remaining colored filters.

© 2001 Buckle Down Publishing Company. DO NOT DUPLICATE.

Color of Crayon	Observations with Filter Color _____	Observations with Filter Color _____	Observations with Filter Color _____	Observations with Filter Color _____

© 2001 Buckle Down Publishing Company. DO NOT DUPLICATE.

Think It Over

1. Review your results from Part 1. Describe the light that was reflected off the colored paper.

    _____

    _____

    _____

2. Based on what you found in Part 1, what happens when you look at a purple sweater? Why does it look purple?

    _____

    _____

    _____

3. How does wearing tinted glasses affect the way you see colors?

    _____

    _____

    _____

© 2001 Buckle Down Publishing Company. DO NOT DUPLICATE.

Practice Questions

Directions: The following diagrams show what happens to a light ray when it hits four different surfaces. Use the diagrams to answer Numbers 1 and 2.

A.    C.

B. 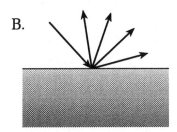   D.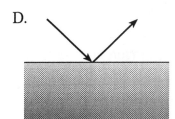

1. Which of these pictures is an example of light being reflected off a rough surface?
   A. A
   B. B
   C. C
   D. D

2. Which of these pictures is an example of refraction?
   A. A
   B. B
   C. C
   D. D

3. Which of the following objects is transparent and colorless?
   A. a piece of glass
   B. a mirror
   C. a plastic milk jug
   D. a sheet of white paper

© 2001 Buckle Down Publishing Company. DO NOT DUPLICATE.

4. On average, men's voices are pitched lower than women's voices. Which of the following statements explains this observation?

   A. Women speak more quickly than men; faster speech is pitched higher.

   B. Women have tighter vocal cords than men; this results in a higher pitch.

   C. Men speak louder than women; the larger amplitude results in a lower pitch.

   D. Men have thicker vocal chords than women; the thicker chords vibrate more slowly, resulting in a lower pitch.

5. Sam yelled across a large canyon and listened for the echo. When she heard the echo, she noticed that her words weren't very clear. Which of the following best describes what took place?

   A. Sam didn't yell loud enough for her voice to carry very far.

   B. The sound waves hit an uneven surface and were scattered.

   C. The rock in the canyon absorbed many of the sound waves.

   D. The air contained a lot of humidity, which reflected the sound waves.

6. Some games have answer cards on which answers are printed in light blue ink. Over the light blue ink, other patterns or words are printed in red. The games have transparent, red plastic filters that the players must put over the answer cards in order to read the answers. Explain how viewing the cards with the filter allows you to read the answer.

   _____

   _____

   _____

   _____

   _____

© 2001 Buckle Down Publishing Company. DO NOT DUPLICATE.

Earth and Space Science

© 2001 Buckle Down Publishing Company. DO NOT DUPLICATE.

Review 18
Rocks

Tracy's lab partner in science, Rick, is a nice guy. He's pretty smart, too, but he doesn't always pay attention. One day last week, the teacher announced, "Tomorrow our subject is types of rock, so make sure you bring everything you'll need."

The next day, Rick showed up with a case full of CDs, his portable CD player, and headphones. "I brought my whole library," he said. "But I don't know what this has to do with science class."

Tracy shook her head. "Not rock and roll—rocks! Igneous, sedimentary, and metamorphic rocks!"

In this review, you'll read about hard rock, soft rock, and all kinds of rock in between. (Feel free to hum along.)

What Do You Think?

There are many different types of rocks and minerals. What do you think the difference is between rocks and minerals? In your explanation, include an example of how rocks and minerals can be used by people.

_____

_____

_____

_____

_____

What People Think

Geologists can provide valuable information to other fields of study, shedding light on environmental conditions and life-forms that existed billions of years ago. An interesting example of this came up recently in western Australia. Scientists discovered what they believe are the oldest rock samples on Earth: 4.4-billion-year-old zircon crystals. Within these crystals, a particular form of oxygen was found that proved that the Earth was cool enough at this time to form liquid water, the

Key Words
erosion
igneous rock
magma
metamorphic rock
mineral
paleontologist
rock
sediment
sedimentary rock
topographical map
weathering

© 2001 Buckle Down Publishing Company. DO NOT DUPLICATE.

first step for the development of life. With this discovery, it appears that the Earth was ready to support life a full 500 million years earlier than previously thought. (That's what Rick might call *classic rock.*)

Minerals are made of pure substances that form naturally as a solid in the Earth. They are usually classified using the characteristics of color, lustre (or shine), streak, and hardness. Examples of minerals include quartz, sulfur, and diamond. **Rocks** are made of a variety of minerals and are classified into three major groups according to the way they were formed: igneous, sedimentary, and metamorphic. Geologists use these characteristics to identify rocks and minerals, to classify them, and to infer how they were formed.

Igneous rocks were born from hot rock—either magma or lava. **Magma** is hot, melted rock below the surface of the Earth; lava is melted rock that flows from active volcanoes and other fractures in the Earth's crust. Geologists often go to places such as Hawaii or Iceland to look for new igneous rocks. The map below shows "hot spots" on the Earth's surface, where volcanoes and earthquakes indicate new igneous rock being produced.

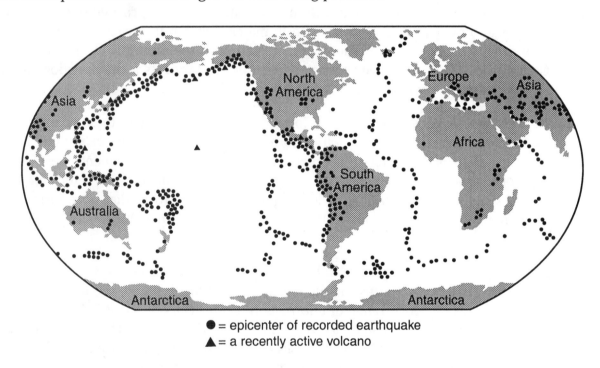

● = epicenter of recorded earthquake
▲ = a recently active volcano

Igneous rocks can be found anywhere, though. At one time, the Earth's surface was covered with active volcanoes. Today, most active volcanoes are located deep below the surface of the oceans, on some islands, and on the "Ring of Fire" around the Pacific Ocean. Can you locate the Ring of Fire on the map?

As lava cools, it forms crystals of common chemical compounds. If the lava is a mixture of different chemical compounds, the resulting igneous rock will be a mixture of different crystallized minerals. The size of the crystal is determined by the cooling rate. Rapid cooling results in small crystals, while slow cooling produces large crystals. Since magma cools below the Earth's surface, it cools slowly; lava cools quickly above the surface.

© 2001 Buckle Down Publishing Company. DO NOT DUPLICATE.

Rhyolite and granite are both igneous rocks. They are made of similar minerals. Rhyolite is fine-grained, while granite is coarse-grained. What is the most likely explanation for the difference?

_____

_____

_____

Once rocks have formed, they are exposed to a variety of environmental conditions. Changing temperatures, from very hot to freezing conditions, cause the rocks to expand and contract. Over time, this causes them to crack and break apart. Rain and wind can also cause rocks to chip and break down into smaller parts. These types of actions are commonly referred to as **weathering**. Glaciers and even plant roots can also weather rock. Some of these materials eventually end up in a river and are carried downstream. **Erosion** is the movement of earth material from one place to another. Along with the rock materials being carried downstream, the moving water also breaks down additional earth material within the river or stream. As the water slows, it drops the materials it carries, which are known as **sediments**. Over time, dissolved chemicals and pressure force sediments together. This process is the basis for the formation of **sedimentary rock**.

Sedimentary rock often looks as if it had been formed in layers. Because of these layers, sedimentary rocks can provide geologists with information about the past. By examining the different strata, or layers, it is possible to approximate how long ago the sediments were deposited. As you saw with the example of the Australian rocks, geologists can determine what the environment was like at a given time by looking at the kinds of rocks that were formed and the size of the grains in these rocks. Using this information makes it possible to study geologic change over time.

Fossils can form within sedimentary rock. **Paleontologists**, as you learned in Review 9, are scientists who study fossils. By determining the location of the fossils within the layers, paleontologists can collect a broad range of information. Fossils can tell scientists what kinds of plants and animals were living during a particular time in the Earth's past. In some situations, the results are surprising. For example, many fossils of ocean animals have been found in the Rocky Mountains. This suggests that the rock that made the mountains was formed at the bottom of an ocean.

Gravity and the constant moving and folding of the Earth's crustal plates brings surface rocks underground again. Heat and pressure beneath the Earth's surface can cause igneous and sedimentary rocks to change. The resulting rock is called **metamorphic rock**. Limestone, a sedimentary rock, changes to marble, a metamorphic rock. Granite, an igneous rock, can change to gneiss (pronounced "nice").

Where within the crust of the Earth would you be most likely to find metamorphic rock?

© 2001 Buckle Down Publishing Company. DO NOT DUPLICATE.

Geologists create special maps to illustrate geological events and relationships. On a typical geology map, each major rock type will have a different visual pattern. People searching for oil, for example, use geology maps to find shale beds, because oil is often found in these formations. In addition, geologists provide a lot of the information that goes into the making of other types of maps. Almost every branch of science—and plenty of areas outside of science—depend on good maps that illustrate geological features. For example, when constructing a new home, a builder will check **topographical maps** of the area (also called *contour maps*) to make sure the home won't be on a floodplain or in the way of possible rockslides. These maps give the changes in elevation by using contour lines; the closer the lines are together, the steeper the slope of the terrain.

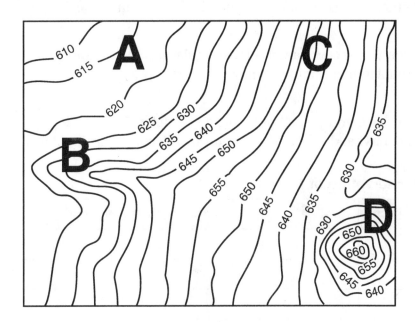

Imagine you are planning a new home with an architect. Looking at this topographical map, decide which of the four spots you would pick for construction. Why?

_____

_____

Check a geology or geography reference textbook for a description of the following specific types of maps. On the lines provided, give a brief account of the purpose of each.

Political maps: _____

Relief maps: _____

Weather maps: _____

Geological maps: _____

Navigation charts: _____

© 2001 Buckle Down Publishing Company. DO NOT DUPLICATE.

Using What You Know

Rocks and minerals come in all shapes and sizes. All rocks and minerals can be grouped and classified, however, using characteristics such as texture, density, color, and crystal size. In this activity, you will take a close look at some rocks and minerals to classify and identify them.

Your teacher will provide you with seven rock samples, labeled from 1 to 7, and a magnifying glass.

Step 1: Place all seven rock samples in front of you. Using the magnifying glass, observe characteristics of each rock. Record your findings in Table 1.

Step 2: Determine which rock samples have similarities to one another. Place them in groups. Keep grouping them until you have three groups.

Step 3: Once you have grouped all of the samples, determine which group is igneous, which is sedimentary, and which is metamorphic. Record your findings in Table 2.

Table 1: Observation of Rocks

Rock Specimen	Characteristics Observed

Table 2: Determining Rock Type

Rock Type	Rock Sample Numbers Belonging to this Group
Igneous	
Metamorphic	
Sedimentary	

© 2001 Buckle Down Publishing Company. DO NOT DUPLICATE.

Think It Over

1. What characteristics are most important in determining which rocks belonged together?

   _____

   _____

   _____

2. What evidence was most helpful in deciding whether a rock was igneous, sedimentary, or metamorphic?

   _____

   _____

   _____

3. Using the characteristics for each rock type, explain the conditions needed to form that type of rock.

   _____

   _____

   _____

   _____

4. There are three rock types but many kinds of rock within each type. Rock types vary because of the different kinds of minerals found in them. Geologists often carry a rock and mineral field guide to aid in identifying individual rocks or minerals. Your teacher will provide you with one of these books.

   For each of the seven rocks used in this investigation, find its scientific name and record it in the space provided.

   Sample 1: _____   Sample 5: _____

   Sample 2: _____   Sample 6: _____

   Sample 3: _____   Sample 7: _____

   Sample 4: _____

© 2001 Buckle Down Publishing Company. DO NOT DUPLICATE.

Practice Questions

1. It can take thousands of years to form certain types of rock. Others form more quickly. What type of rock could have been formed since the year in which you were born?

    A. igneous

    B. diamond

    C. sedimentary

    D. metamorphic

2. What type of rock would be most likely to contain fossils?

    A. granite

    B. igneous

    C. sedimentary

    D. metamorphic

3. Rock climbing has become popular in the last decade. Many large rocks are not suitable for this sport, though. Climbers recommend avoiding limestone cliffs because the rock is

    A. too hard to get a grip on.

    B. formed too close to active volcanoes.

    C. made of material that is easy to break.

    D. full of extremely sharp crystals that can cut rope.

4. Why is sedimentary rock a good rock to study when investigating geologic changes over time?

    _____

    _____

    _____

5. What is the difference between a rock and a mineral?

    _____

    _____

    _____

6. Which of the situations below would not lead directly to the formation of sedimentary rock?

    A. A landslide spills into a nearby river.

    B. A volcanic eruption creates a lava flow.

    C. Rock eroded by tree roots is swept into a river.

    D. Melted water from a glacier flows down a mountain and into a river.

© 2001 Buckle Down Publishing Company. DO NOT DUPLICATE.

Review 19
Human Activity and the Earth's Surface

Natural events such as rain, wind, river flow, temperature change, and atmospheric change have been occurring since the Earth was first formed. These events continually act upon the Earth's surface. Over long periods of time, even slow processes can have enormous effects.

Human activity also can have significant effects on the Earth. In this review, you will learn about the impact of people on the rate of some natural processes, particularly erosion.

What Do You Think?

Have you ever been to the Grand Canyon? Below is an illustration of a small portion of this national treasure.

How do you think such a large canyon was formed?

_____

_____

_____

_____

_____

_____

_____

Key Words
chemical weathering
erosion
irrigation
ore
physical weathering
reclamation
surface mining

© 2001 Buckle Down Publishing Company. DO NOT DUPLICATE.

What People Think

Because our own life spans are so short compared to geological history, the changes that everyday weather conditions may cause over thousands and millions of years are hard to imagine. Occasionally, though, events occur that make it clear how weathering can cause significant changes to the Earth's surface.

Perhaps on the news or in your own community, you have seen the effects of flash flooding. Flash floods occur when extraordinarily heavy rain falls in an area. Rivers and streams overflow their banks suddenly and then move rapidly across the landscape.

What happens to the landscape in a flash flood?

_____

_____

_____

What happens to the material that is missing from an area after a flash flood?

_____

_____

_____

Water typically moves much more slowly in normal circumstances than in flooding situations. What might be the effects of slowly moving water during a short period of time, such as several hours? What might be the effects of slowly moving water over millions of years?

_____

_____

_____

_____

© 2001 Buckle Down Publishing Company. DO NOT DUPLICATE.

Physical weathering occurs when rocks are broken into smaller pieces through exposure to temperature changes (especially freeze/thaw cycles), glaciers, running water, growing roots, and certain human activities (like farming and road construction). Rock can also be broken down chemically. **Chemical weathering** is caused by exposure to elements such as rain and surface water, oxygen and other gases in the atmosphere, substances given off by organisms, and human pollution.

The processes by which earth material is broken down and moved from one place to another is called **erosion**. Natural erosion, which has slowly occurred since the Earth formed 5 billion years ago, is mostly beneficial because it results in the formation of new soil. But the rate of erosion has greatly increased because of human activities, such as poor farming practices, logging, construction, and mining. These activities can actually result in the loss of soil.

How can human activities increase the rate of erosion?

_____

_____

_____

Humans alter our environment in other ways. We use the Earth's soil to meet our daily nutritional needs by growing food or raising animals. Frequently, this is done on land that needs **irrigation**, which puts extra demands on the water resources. Plants also are used to meet human needs, and the removal of them alters the environment. For example, when trees are harvested, it takes many years, often decades, before new trees can grow to the same size. Clear-cutting forests leads to increased carbon dioxide levels in the atmosphere (you learned about the photosynthesis/respiration cycle in Review 7), and it opens the sides of mountains to erosion and destructive landslides.

In addition, humans can alter the environment through such things as urban developments, landfills, and sewage disposal. All of these things are required for humans to live comfortably. We need houses to live in, so we build more houses. One of the impacts of these developments is that the houses cover up valuable farming land. We also produce both garbage and human waste. In Review 15, you learned that we usually get rid of garbage by burying it in large holes in the ground. Not only does this change the surface of the ground, it can affect the surrounding area. Toxic chemicals can leak out and spread into the nearby soil, groundwater, and rivers. This may cause the chemicals to be transported many miles from the landfill. Human waste or sewage must also be disposed of. Usually, this occurs by dumping the waste into water or on the ground. Sometimes the sewage is treated, but sometimes it is not, which causes many health problems.

© 2001 Buckle Down Publishing Company. DO NOT DUPLICATE.

A variety of nonliving resources are extracted from the ground. List two or three different nonliving resources that humans use.

_____

_____

_____

In your list, you probably identified nonliving resources such as petroleum products—oil and natural gas—and minerals such as coal and iron. Oil and gas are vital resources to the United States. Approximately 40% of all the energy used in this country comes from oil and 23% comes from natural gas.

What types of technologies use these two types of resources?

_____

_____

_____

Mining is another way humans can alter the surface of the Earth. **Surface mining**, also called strip mining or open-pit mining, involves extracting minerals that are buried underground but near the Earth's surface. About 90% of all minerals are mined in this way in the United States. In Michigan, mining companies use surface mining to extract iron, portland cement, and copper, among other things. Surface mining is done by having huge equipment remove the soil, rock, and vegetation that cover the minerals. This material, called *overburden*, is then placed to the side. The mineral **ore** can then be extracted from the ground. The mineral ore contains a mixture of various rocks and the mineral or mineral compounds being mined. The *refining* process removes the mineral from the rock and purifies it. During this process, a lot of energy is used, and air and water pollution can result. The solid-waste material, or *tailings*, that remain after refining can be especially hard to dispose of in an environmentally safe manner. Mining companies are expected to restore or reclaim the land, bringing it back to its original state. The **reclamation** process involves putting the overburden back in the ground and replanting the vegetation. One particularly sensitive area in Michigan, the dunes along Lake Michigan, have been endangered by sand mining companies. State and local efforts have resulted in laws that require the companies to reclaim the areas that have been mined.

© 2001 Buckle Down Publishing Company. DO NOT DUPLICATE.

Using What You Know

In this activity, you will be creating a model of a mining project. Scientists often use models to simulate events that would be very difficult or expensive to stage in reality. Your model of the mining project will require you to extract a resource using the surface mining technique and then to reclaim the land.

Part 1 – Construct the Model

Step 1: To make the mining model, your teacher will give you the appropriate materials.

Step 2: Place about 2 inches of sand in the bottom of your pan.

Step 3: Place your mineral resources (marbles) anywhere in the pan.

Step 4: Cover the minerals with about 2 inches more sand.

Step 5: Cover the sand with about 0.5 inches of soil.

Step 6: Cover the top of the soil with grass, leaves, or similar materials.

Part 2 – Mine Your Resources and Reclaim the Mine Site

Step 1: Your teacher will give you the appropriate mining tools. Note how each tool represents a different type of technology. For example, the spoon will probably be used for digging, the tweezers can be used for removing and planting grass and leaves, and the wooden stick may be used to probe for the minerals.

Step 2: You have the following four tasks to complete.

- Locate the mineral.
- Mine the mineral.
- Separate the mineral from the other materials.
- Safely dispose of any waste, and reclaim the mining site.

© 2001 Buckle Down Publishing Company. DO NOT DUPLICATE.

Step 3: Draw your mining site as it looks before you start mining.

Step 4: Begin mining when your teacher directs you to start. For each action you take, record what you did, the different materials or technologies you used, and the number of minerals you collected. Also, be sure to keep a record of changes in soil depth and vegetation coverage.

Step 5: When you are done mining the resource, reclaim the mining site.

Step 6: Draw your reclaimed mining site.

© 2001 Buckle Down Publishing Company. DO NOT DUPLICATE.

Think It Over

1. In what ways was this activity similar to surface mining?

   _____

   _____

   _____

   How was it different?

   _____

   _____

   _____

2. List the types of materials or technologies you used at each of the following stages in the mining process.

   a) Exploration: _____

   _____

   b) Removal of mineral: _____

   _____

   c) Reclamation: _____

   _____

3. List at least one environmental impact or problem at each of the following stages.

   a) Removal and storage of the overburden: _____

   _____

   b) Removal of the mineral: _____

   _____

   c) Reclamation: _____

   _____

© 2001 Buckle Down Publishing Company. DO NOT DUPLICATE.

4. Compare your two drawings of the mining site. How are they the same? How are they different?

_____

_____

_____

5. Is it possible to restore the land to the exact same conditions that existed before the mining started? Is this an important thing to be able to do? Explain your answer.

_____

_____

_____

_____

Practice Questions

Directions: Use the following illustrations to answer Numbers 1 and 2.

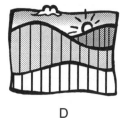

| A | B | C | D |

1. The lines in the illustrations above represent rows of crops. Which way of growing crops will result in the least erosion?

   A. A   C. C
   B. B   D. D

2. Which way of growing crops will result in the most erosion?

   A. A   C. C
   B. B   D. D

© 2001 Buckle Down Publishing Company. DO NOT DUPLICATE.

3. Complete the following statement: Erosion is
   A. a natural process that is affected by some human actions.
   B. a natural process that is caused only by rapidly moving water.
   C. an unnatural process that must be stopped wherever it occurs.
   D. an unnatural process that is caused primarily by human actions.

4. Walking in the park one afternoon, you see a large copper statue of a horseback rider that has turned blue-green from exposure to the air. You notice that streaks of this blue-green substance have stained the concrete pedestal of the statue, as chemical compounds in the rain have reacted with the statue's copper. This is an example of
   A. mineral extraction.
   B. copper reclamation.
   C. physical weathering.
   D. chemical weathering.

5. Describe three different examples of how humans use technology to change the surface of the Earth.

   _____

   _____

   _____

   _____

6. Minerals are mined to make products that we buy. How do our buying habits affect mining? How can you reduce the need to mine so many minerals?

   _____

   _____

   _____

   _____

   _____

   _____

© 2001 Buckle Down Publishing Company. DO NOT DUPLICATE.

Review 20
Water, the Universal Molecule

Three-quarters of our planet is covered with water. Only about 3% of it is freshwater, however. Human, plant, and animal life must share that tiny amount of freshwater. Many of us never stop to think about what water really is or about its unique properties. This review will help you understand why water is sometimes called the "universal molecule."

What Do You Think?

As you learned in Review 12, the water molecule is made up of two hydrogen atoms and one oxygen atom. Its chemical formula is H_2O.

Name some other characteristics of water.

_____

_____

_____

Even though water is the universal molecule, bottled water is more expensive than gasoline! Why do you think bottled water is becoming so popular?

_____

_____

_____

What People Think

You could call Earth "the Water Planet." There's water in the atmosphere, on the surface, and underground. As you learned in Review 15, about 97.2% of the Earth's water is in the oceans in the form of undrinkable saltwater. The rest is flowing in lakes, rivers, and wetlands, frozen in glaciers, and pooled under the surface of the Earth. Water that soaks into the Earth is called **groundwater**. During the last Ice Age, much of the Earth's freshwater was captured in the glaciers that covered North America. As the glaciers melted and receded, water was deposited into many of the lakes and wetlands that dot the Michigan landscape. Freshwater supports all life on Earth.

Key Words
aquifer

condensation

evaporation

groundwater

humidity

precipitation

runoff

water cycle

© 2001 Buckle Down Publishing Company. DO NOT DUPLICATE.

If global warming continues, more of the glaciers and the polar ice caps will melt, raising the level of the oceans. Rather than forming lakes and wetlands, this melted ice will be lost to the saltwater oceans.

Even though three-quarters of the Earth's surface is covered by water, water shortages are a growing problem. Why?

_____

_____

No new water is being created by nature. What we have is recycled forever through the water cycle. The **water cycle** is a name for the circular process water goes through. Water from oceans and other bodies of water is heated by the Sun until it becomes a gas and goes into the atmosphere (**evaporation**) as water vapor. The amount of water vapor in the air is the air's **humidity**. The water vapor rises and eventually cools, becoming a liquid again (**condensation**) and forming clouds. Then it falls back to the ground as some form of **precipitation**. Precipitation that isn't absorbed into the ground or evaporated flows to waterways as **runoff**. Then the whole process starts over again. The type of precipitation that falls depends on the temperature of the upper atmosphere and the surface of the Earth. The water cycle naturally moves water from place to place and keeps it pure.

List as many forms of precipitation as you can.

_____

_____

Put the labels *evaporation*, *condensation*, *precipitation*, and *runoff* in the appropriate places in the following diagram of the water cycle.

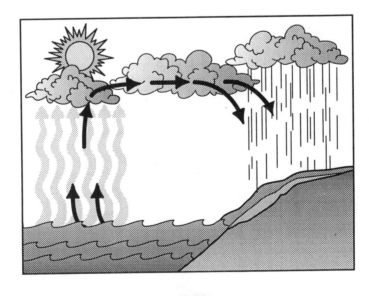

© 2001 Buckle Down Publishing Company. DO NOT DUPLICATE.

Water from precipitation has two places to go: It can either run off the land or soak into it. Most water ends up as runoff. Runoff water goes into lakes and rivers. Most of it eventually ends up in the oceans. When large amounts of groundwater are stored in porous rock, like sandstone, an **aquifer** is formed. Aquifers are usually the source of water for wells.

Using the map below, describe or trace a route that melted snow could possibly travel to get to the Atlantic Ocean.

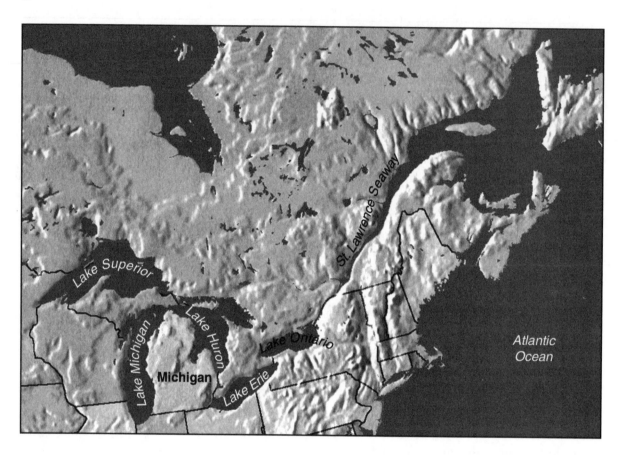

© 2001 Buckle Down Publishing Company. DO NOT DUPLICATE.

Using What You Know

In this activity, you will construct a model to represent all the water found on our planet Earth. You will need a 1-liter container, salt, water, an eyedropper, and access to a freezer.

Step 1: Fill a 1-liter container with water. This represents all the water found on Earth.

Step 2: Take out 30 ml of water and place to the side. Add about 29 g of salt to the 970 ml of water in the container. This represents all the saltwater in the oceans.

Step 3: Take 23 ml of water out of the 30 ml of water you put to the side and place it in the freezer. This represents all the water in the glaciers and ice caps.

Step 4: The remaining 7 ml represents all the freshwater on Earth. Take an eyedropper and place one drop of the freshwater in your hand. This one drop represents all the freshwater available to humans for drinking purposes.

Step 5: Make a chart in the space provided below to illustrate Steps 1 through 4.

© 2001 Buckle Down Publishing Company. DO NOT DUPLICATE.

Think It Over

1. What percentage of the total water on Earth is freshwater?

    _____

    _____

2. What percentage of the total water on Earth is saltwater?

    _____

    _____

3. Why is drinking water considered such a precious resource?

    _____

    _____

4. If you were told that someone was polluting the area around your drinking water, what would be your response to this problem?

    _____

    _____

    _____

© 2001 Buckle Down Publishing Company. DO NOT DUPLICATE.

Practice Questions

1. Which item below is not part of the water cycle?
   A. condensation
   B. precipitation
   C. evaporation
   D. calcification

2. To use ocean water for drinking purposes, humans must
   A. add more salt to it.
   B. put it in bottles or cans.
   C. remove the salt from it.
   D. ship it to areas that need water most.

3. Which of the following pathways best describes how water could get from Michigan to the Atlantic Ocean?
   A. Michigan, St. Lawrence Seaway, Atlantic Ocean
   B. Michigan, Great Lakes, St. Lawrence Seaway, Atlantic Ocean
   C. Michigan, St. Lawrence Seaway, Great Lakes, Atlantic Ocean
   D. Michigan, Great Lakes, Atlantic Ocean

4. Describe two different forms water can take on our planet and indicate the conditions under which these two forms occur.

   _____

   _____

   _____

5. What is the difference between groundwater and surface water?

   _____

   _____

   _____

© 2001 Buckle Down Publishing Company. DO NOT DUPLICATE.

Review 21
Earth's Atmosphere

When you wake up each morning, do you look out the window to see what the weather is like? If you do, you are not alone. Weather affects everyone in many different ways; it determines what clothes you put on in the morning, what crops a farmer plants each spring, and when to plan for a picnic. **Meteorologists** are scientists trained to observe and predict weather conditions. They also look for patterns in weather over long periods of time, and they speculate about the causes of certain weather conditions. In this review, you will learn more about the factors these professionals study to create accurate forecasts.

What Do You Think?

You know that it is warm and sunny in the tropics and cold and dreary in the Arctic and Antarctic regions of the Earth, but the same Sun shines all over the Earth.

Why do the tropics and polar regions have such different weather?

_____

_____

_____

A weather reporter on television states, "There is no weather today." Is this possible? What does the weather reporter mean to say?

_____

_____

_____

_____

_____

_____

_____

Key Words

air pressure

differential heating effect

exosphere

ionosphere

mesosphere

meteorologist

stratosphere

thermosphere

troposphere

water cycle

© 2001 Buckle Down Publishing Company. DO NOT DUPLICATE.

What People Think

The atmosphere is arranged in five layers. The first layer, the **troposphere**, goes from the Earth's surface to an altitude of 11 km. The composition of the air in this layer is about 78% nitrogen, 21% oxygen, and 1% other gases. Most aircraft fly within this layer, and weather occurs only in this layer. The second layer of the atmosphere is the **stratosphere**. It is about 37 km thick and is located 11 km to 48 km above the Earth's surface. Only specialized supersonic jets can fly this high. This layer contains the ozone that absorbs much of the harmful radiation from the Sun. The third layer, the **mesosphere**, stretches from about 48 km to 88 km above the Earth's surface. The **thermosphere** is much thicker, extending from 88 km to 700 km above the Earth's surface. Space shuttles and the International Space Station orbit the Earth in this layer. The mesosphere and part of the thermosphere are sometimes called the **ionosphere** because of the number of free electrons and ions present. The outer layer of the atmosphere is called the **exosphere** and begins at 700 km above the Earth's surface. Satellites that orbit Earth can be found here. Not all scientists agree about the specific altitudes of each layer—where one begins and the next one ends—so look at the numbers in this diagram as "best-fit" estimates.

Layers of the Earth's Atmosphere

exosphere

435 miles (700 km)

thermosphere

250 miles (402 km)

ionosphere

55 miles (88 km)

mesosphere

30 miles (48 km)

stratosphere

ozone layer

7 miles (11 km)

troposphere

(Drawing not to scale)

© 2001 Buckle Down Publishing Company. DO NOT DUPLICATE.

The mistake that the weather reporter made earlier was to think that "no weather" meant the same thing as "calm weather." There is always weather, which is defined as conditions in the troposphere at any given moment. Weather is the result of complex interactions between the Sun, the Earth, and the Earth's atmosphere. The Sun's radiation, or energy, drives the weather by unevenly heating the Earth's land, water, and air. This differential heating, as well as the **water cycle** (which you learned about in Review 20), the Earth's tilting, and the Earth's rotation, help explain most weather events.

What are some major components of weather? (Hint: Recalling the topics of a recent weather report may help you answer this question.)

_____

_____

_____

You learned about the water cycle in Review 20. The type of precipitation that falls depends on the temperature of the upper atmosphere and the surface of the Earth. If the temperature close to the ground is below 0° C, the precipitation is snow. If the temperature is above 0° C, the precipitation is rain. If the upper atmosphere is below zero, sometimes water freezes around a dust particle in the atmosphere and forms a small ice ball. Sometimes the ice ball doesn't fall to the ground but is blown back up into the clouds. If this process is repeated, hailstones of various sizes can fall to the ground. Hailstones usually have a diameter of about 1 to 2 cm, but can sometimes be as large as 12–13 cm.

As Earth travels around the Sun, it is not straight up and down on its axis of rotation (the imaginary line running between the North Pole and the South Pole). Instead, it is tilted at an angle of 23.5°, which causes different regions of the Earth to be heated differently. This difference, combined with the fact that sand, rock, soil, vegetation, and water take different amounts of energy to heat, is called the **differential heating effect**. Differential heating of the Earth causes air to move and circulate. It also contributes to the formation of clouds. Warm air is lighter than cool air, so when the Sun heats an area of the ground, the air in that area rises. Cool air comes in to take its place, and a current is set up. As the warmed air rises, it cools and eventually condenses to form clouds. Clouds also form when air lifts as it moves over hills or mountains, as well as when a mass of warm air meets a mass of cool air.

How do people flying gliders and hang gliders use these properties of warm and cool air to keep their aircraft aloft?

_____

_____

_____

© 2001 Buckle Down Publishing Company. DO NOT DUPLICATE.

Meteorologists name clouds based upon their shape and the height at which they form. Clouds that appear the highest in the sky generally have the prefix *cirro-*, which means *wisp* or *curl.* Cirrus clouds are high, wispy, white clouds, and they do not produce precipitation that reaches the ground. Clouds in the middle height range usually have the terms *cumulo-* (meaning *heap* or *pile*) or *strato-* (meaning *spread-out* or *sheetlike*). Cumulus clouds form puffy white piles and sometimes bring brief showers. Cumulonimbus clouds rise from a dark bottom to a tall white top and usually bring thunderstorms. Altostratus clouds cover the sky in a smooth white or gray sheet, but their moisture usually doesn't reach the ground. Clouds at the lowest levels are usually some type of stratus clouds, and they often bring a drizzle.

How does cloud cover affect a region's temperature during the day?

_____

_____

How does cloud cover affect a region's temperature at night?

_____

_____

Meteorologists use a variety of tools to measure the weather. Thermometers are used to determine local temperature. Barometers are used to measure the amount of **air pressure** in the atmosphere. High-pressure systems generally bring fair weather. Low-pressure systems usually bring cloudy, unstable conditions. In the United States, these high- and low-pressure systems usually travel from west to east. Measuring the barometric pressure is an important factor in explaining the current weather conditions and in predicting future weather.

Imagine that you are watching a weather forecast, and the meteorologist says that your region should expect the current low-pressure system to move out and be replaced by a high-pressure system. What type of weather are you having and how will it change?

_____

_____

© 2001 Buckle Down Publishing Company. DO NOT DUPLICATE.

Using What You Know

Winds are created by differences in air pressure. When areas of high pressure come into contact with low-pressure areas, the air from the high-pressure area moves into the low-pressure area, resulting in wind. In the following activity, you will explore the causes and patterns of wind.

Look at the following three diagrams. Diagram 1 shows a high-pressure system over Traverse City (in northwest Michigan) and a low-pressure system over Detroit. Between the two cities are three weather stations that can measure wind speed: one just outside of Traverse City, one just outside of Detroit, and one halfway between the two cities. Diagram 2 shows the high-pressure system moving over weather station 2 and the low-pressure system moving out into Lake Erie. Diagram 3 shows the high-pressure system moving over Detroit.

Directions: Describe the wind speed at the three weather stations in each diagram. Use the following terms: *calm*, *light winds*, and *strong winds*.

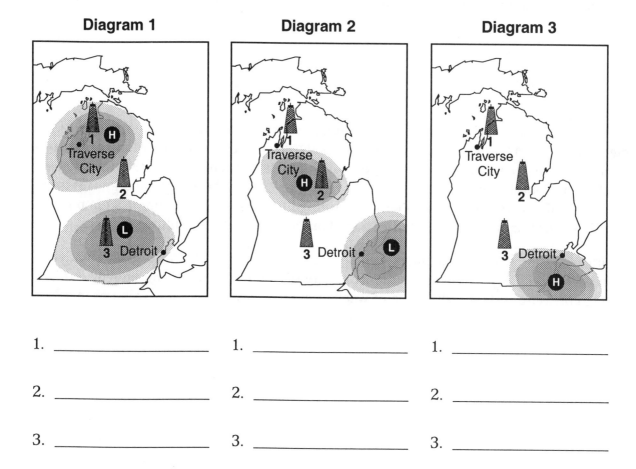

Diagram 1   Diagram 2   Diagram 3

1. _____   1. _____   1. _____

2. _____   2. _____   2. _____

3. _____   3. _____   3. _____

© 2001 Buckle Down Publishing Company. DO NOT DUPLICATE.

Think It Over

1. Using the three diagrams as a guide, describe the direction of the wind. Support your answer.

   _____

   _____

   _____

2. Which way does the wind blow—from high to low pressure, or low to high pressure?

   _____

   _____

   _____

3. Describe what the wind speed would be at each weather station if there were a fourth diagram.

   _____

   _____

   _____

© 2001 Buckle Down Publishing Company. DO NOT DUPLICATE.

Practice Questions

1. In what layer of the atmosphere does weather occur?
   A. exosphere
   B. ionosphere
   C. stratosphere
   D. troposphere

2. Starting from the base of a mountain, you climb to the top while carrying a barometer. How will the barometer reading at the top of the mountain compare to the reading at the bottom of the mountain?
   A. higher
   B. lower
   C. the same
   D. zero

3. As you go up or down a mountain, what causes the "popping" that you may feel in your ears?
   A. a change in elevation
   B. a change in temperature
   C. a difference in pressure inside and outside your ears
   D. a difference in humidity inside your ears and in the atmosphere

Directions: Use the following illustration to answer Numbers 4 and 5.

A. Cumulus   B. Stratus   C. Cirrus   D. Cumulonimbus

4. Which type of cloud is most often associated with thunderstorms?
   A. A   C. C
   B. B   D. D

5. Which type of cloud usually indicates fair weather?
   A. A   C. C
   B. B   D. D

© 2001 Buckle Down Publishing Company. DO NOT DUPLICATE.

Review 22
Spaceship Earth in the Solar System

Throughout our existence, human beings have taken great risks and overcome incredible obstacles to explore new places on Earth. Today, we are taking new risks and overcoming ever-more challenging obstacles to venture out into our solar system. During the past 50 years, our understanding of space has deepened greatly, thanks in part to new technologies, including *Hubble Space Telescope*, satellite probes, robots, space shuttles, and computerized imaging. All of these technologies have contributed pieces to the puzzle of the structure and workings of the solar system and the rest of the universe. This review will give you a chance to explore some of the things we know about our universe and our solar system.

What Do You Think?

Usually when you write a letter or send an e-mail, there is some form of return address. This tells the receiver who sent the message. Imagine you are sending a message to another part of our universe. Using the following terms, write your return address in the correct order: *United States of America, Milky Way Galaxy, your name, North America, your street address, Planet Earth, the Universe, your town, Solar System, Michigan.*

Key Words

orbit

phase

revolve

rotate

solar system

universe

© 2001 Buckle Down Publishing Company. DO NOT DUPLICATE.

What People Think

Our **solar system**, with its central star—the Sun—and the nine planets and their moons, is located in the Milky Way galaxy. Our galaxy is one of billions in the **universe**. Everything is moving! The universe is expanding, the galaxies are spinning, and the planets and moons are rotating and revolving. It is important that you realize that these motions combine to produce a very complex and dynamic universe.

Find a map of the Milky Way Galaxy in a reference book. Sketch or describe the location of our solar system within the galaxy in the space below.

All of the objects in our solar system **revolve** in an **orbit** around our closest star, the Sun. Although the Sun isn't all that big by the standards of the universe, it's huge compared to the planets that revolve around it. If you were to add up the entire mass of the solar system—the Sun, all nine planets, their moons, the comets and asteroids, dust, and gases—the Sun would make up 99.86% of the total mass of the system.

© 2001 Buckle Down Publishing Company. DO NOT DUPLICATE.

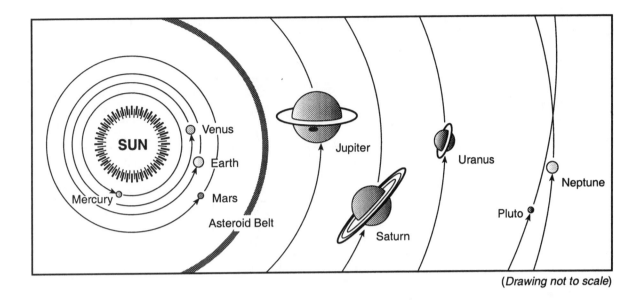

(*Drawing not to scale*)

If you have ever attended a school science fair, you may have seen a model of our solar system in a cardboard box diorama. What might be wrong with the model's magnitude and scale?

_____

_____

_____

The four planets closest to the Sun are called *terrestrial planets*. *Terrestrial* is a term used to describe the planets most like Earth. The next four planets are gaseous and have thick, swirling atmospheres. The last, Pluto, is similar in composition to the terrestrial planets. Pluto occasionally drifts within the orbit of Neptune, as you can see from the solar system diagram above.

We are able to tell the planets apart in the sky by their size, shape, color, brightness, and movement. In addition, we can distinguish the planets by the number of moons orbiting them. All of the planets except Mercury and Venus have moons. Earth has only one moon, whereas Saturn has at least twenty. Each planet **rotates**, or spins, on its axis as it revolves around the Sun.

© 2001 Buckle Down Publishing Company. DO NOT DUPLICATE.

Using the table of planetary characteristics below, list three other characteristics that make Earth unique.

Planet	Period of Rotation	Number of Moons	Diameter (km)	Period of Revolution in Earth Time
Mercury	59.0 days	0	4,880	88.0 days
Venus	243.0 days	0	12,100	225.0 days
Earth	24.0 hours	1	12,750	365.25 days
Mars	24.6 hours	2	6,790	687.0 days
Jupiter	10.0 hours	16	142,700	11.8 years
Saturn	10.6 hours	23	120,000	29.5 years
Uranus	16.5 hours	15	50,800	84.0 years
Neptune	16.0 hours	8	48,600	164.8 years
Pluto	9.5 hours	1	2,300	247.7 years

_____

_____

_____

_____

_____

Using the terms *revolve*, *rotate*, and *axis*, explain why one year on Earth is about 365 days long and why one day on Earth is 24 hours long.

_____

_____

_____

© 2001 Buckle Down Publishing Company. DO NOT DUPLICATE.

Earth's characteristics—its periods of rotation and revolution, distance from the Sun, rocky composition, and so on—all add up to provide the one, big characteristic that we think is unique to Earth: the ability to support life. Just the right balance of temperature, gravity, age, and chemical composition allowed water to develop on Earth. As you learned in Review 20, water is *the* essential ingredient of life, maybe even more important than sunlight. Scientists think that our best chance for finding life outside of Earth would be on one of Jupiter's moons, Europa. Europa is completely covered in ice. Underneath that, astronomers think, is a vast ocean of water, covering the entire moon, that is kept warm by volcanic action. Deep-sea scientists on Earth have discovered unique organisms at the bottom of the ocean floor that don't seem to need sunlight to live: They get their energy from chemical reactions with volcanic gases. So, could life have formed in volcanic oceans on Europa? We'll have to wait a long time to see, but it is an exciting prospect.

Pick one planet besides Earth and imagine that we have discovered a life form there. What would your life-form look like? Be sure to relate your creature's form to its planet's characteristics.

_____

_____

_____

_____

_____

You know why Earth has day and night, but what about the seasons? Many people believe the seasons are caused by the elliptic shape of the Earth's orbit. Actually, the Earth's orbit is nearly circular. The slight difference in the distance to the Sun cannot explain the seasons. In fact, the Earth is closer to the Sun during winter in the northern hemisphere than during summer in the northern hemisphere. Earth's axis is tilted at an angle of about 23.5°. The four seasons—spring, summer, fall, and winter—are caused by this tilt. For example, Earth's Northern Hemisphere experiences the most sunlight in a day on June 20 or 21 each year, when summer begins; the Southern Hemisphere experiences the least sunlight on that day. This is because on June 20 or 21, the Earth is at the point in its orbit around the Sun in which the Northern Hemisphere is tilted farthest toward the Sun, and the Southern Hemisphere is tilted its farthest away from the Sun. The following diagram shows how the tilting causes the seasons.

© 2001 Buckle Down Publishing Company. DO NOT DUPLICATE.

Earth's Orbit Around the Sun

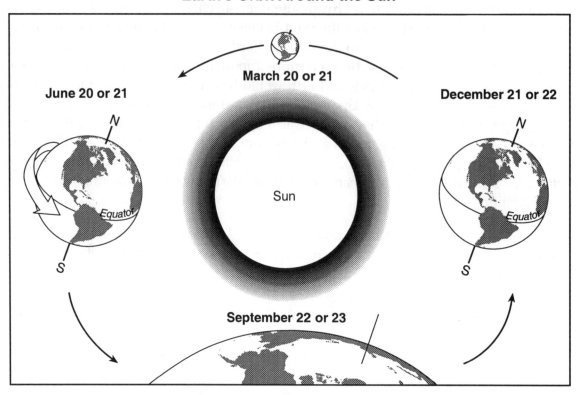

The force of gravity keeps the planets in their orbits around the Sun. The speed of the planets as they travel through space keeps them moving forward. The Sun's gravity, however, pulls the planets toward it, keeping the planets from flying out of their orbits and out of the solar system.

Imagine that you are twirling a yo-yo on the end of a string looped around your finger. How are the forces caused by twirling the yo-yo in a big circle similar to the forces involved with planets orbiting the Sun? What forces are involved?

_____

_____

_____

_____

Gravity keeps the Moon revolving around the Earth, and the Moon's gravitational attraction is the main cause of Earth's ocean tides. It takes the Moon just over 27 days to make a complete orbit of the Earth. During this orbit, the Moon's shape, as seen from Earth, goes through **phases**: from new moon to first quarter, full moon, last quarter, and back to new moon.

© 2001 Buckle Down Publishing Company. DO NOT DUPLICATE.

The rotation of the Earth makes it appear that other objects in space are moving around us. Our rotation makes the Sun appear to rise and set every day, and it even makes the stars appear to move through the night sky. It is easy to see why ancient people believed that the Earth was the center of the universe. However, the stars and the Sun are essentially standing still (they do not orbit other bodies), whereas planets and other bodies, such as comets and asteroids, move around them. Astronomers can tell that the other planets of our solar system are moving by studying how the positions of the planets change in relation to each other and to the position of the stars.

Why can we usually only see one or two other planets in the night sky? (Hint: Look at the diagram on page 181 and think about how long it takes for each of those planets to make one revolution around the Sun.)

_____

_____

_____

_____

Using What You Know

Now that you know about the motions of the Earth, Moon, and Sun, it's time to create a model illustrating the phases of the Moon. For this activity, you will need a large ball to represent the Earth, a small ball to represent the Moon, and a flashlight to represent the Sun. You may work in groups of four.

Step 1: Demonstrate and describe, with the large ball, the Earth rotating on its axis. Remember, the Earth rotates in a west-to-east direction (counterclockwise).

_____

_____

Step 2: Demonstrate and describe, with the large ball and flashlight, the Earth's orbit as it revolves around the Sun.

_____

_____

_____

© 2001 Buckle Down Publishing Company. DO NOT DUPLICATE.

Step 3: Describe how your model of the Earth orbiting the Sun can explain the seasons.

_____

_____

_____

Step 4: Demonstrate and describe, with both balls, the motion of the Moon orbiting the Earth.

_____

_____

Step 5: Demonstrate how a full moon occurs. Illustrate your results.

Step 6: A new moon occurs when the moon is not visible in the sky at night. Arrange your Earth, Moon, and Sun to demonstrate how a new moon occurs every month. Illustrate your results.

© 2001 Buckle Down Publishing Company. DO NOT DUPLICATE.

Think It Over

1. In terms of how the Earth moves, what is the difference between a day and a year?

    _____

    _____

2. Looking at the positions of the Sun, Earth, and Moon, what is the difference between a new moon and a full moon?

    _____

    _____

3. Illustrate how you think the Sun, Earth, and Moon would have to be aligned to create a lunar eclipse. How is a solar eclipse different?

    _____

    _____

4. When we see the Moon, light is being reflected off the Moon's surface. Where does this light come from?

    _____

    _____

© 2001 Buckle Down Publishing Company. DO NOT DUPLICATE.

Practice Questions

1. Which of the following statements is correct?

   A. The Moon revolves around Earth, and Earth revolves around the Sun.

   B. Earth rotates around the Moon, and the Moon rotates around the Sun.

   C. Earth revolves around the Moon, and the Moon revolves around the Sun.

   D. The Moon rotates around Earth, and Earth rotates around the Sun.

2. The seasons are caused by

   A. a shift in the tilt of the Earth's axis.

   B. the distance of the Earth from the Sun.

   C. the tilt of the Earth relative to the Sun.

   D. the position of the Earth relative to the Moon.

3. Shown here are pictures of four of the Moon's phases. Also shown here is a diagram of the Sun and the Earth, as well as the Moon in four different positions as it revolves around the Earth. Study the diagrams, then match the position of the Moon with the phase that people on Earth see.

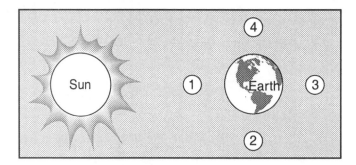

| New Moon | First Quarter | Full Moon | Last Quarter |

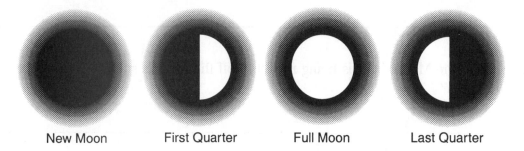

Position 1—Phase: _New Moon_

Position 2—Phase: _First quarter_

Position 3—Phase: _full moon_

Position 4—Phase: _last quarter_

© 2001 Buckle Down Publishing Company. DO NOT DUPLICATE.

4. As you know, the Earth's ocean tides are mainly caused by the Moon. Do you think the highest tides occur when there is a new or full moon, or when there is a first or last quarter moon? Explain why you think this.

_____

_____

_____

5. Explain how gravity keeps the planets orbiting the Sun, and how it keeps the Moon orbiting the Earth.

_____

_____

_____

_____

6. Which of the following lists is in the correct order from smallest to largest?
   A. Earth, Sun, our solar system, Milky Way
   B. our solar system, Milky Way, Earth, Sun
   C. Sun, Milky Way, our solar system, Earth
   D. Milky Way, our solar system, Sun, Earth

© 2001 Buckle Down Publishing Company. DO NOT DUPLICATE.

PEOPLE IN SCIENCE

Subrahmanyan Chandrasekhar
(CHAN-dra-SEK-har)
(India 1910–1995)

In 1930, Subrahmanyan Chandrasekhar was sailing to England from his home in India. He was about to study astronomy at the University of Cambridge. On the boat ride, he studied the vivid night skies filled with stars. He started to think about the life span of those stars and what happens when they die. When a star runs out of fuel to burn, it either explodes or collapses. When the latter happens, then what? Chandrasekhar combined his knowledge of physics and mathematics and came to a startling conclusion. A star collapses to become one of two things: Stars smaller than 1.45 times the size of our Sun become white dwarfs, and stars larger than this become black holes. A white dwarf is a collapsed star that still shines because its gravitational energy is converted to heat. A black hole is a collapsed star with so much concentrated gravity that nothing, not even light, can escape. Chandrasekhar's boat ride led to a career filled with discovery. He graduated from Cambridge and moved to America, where he taught at the University of Chicago. For his work in astronomy, he was awarded the Nobel Prize for physics in 1983. Recently, a spacecraft was even named after him: *Chandra X-ray Observatory* went into orbit in 1999.

© 2001 Buckle Down Publishing Company. DO NOT DUPLICATE.

appendix

Glossary

Michigan Science Content Standards and
Benchmarks — Middle School

© 2001 Buckle Down Publishing Company. DO NOT DUPLICATE.

Glossary

abiotic: of or relating to nonliving things (Review 10)

absorb: to soak up, like a sponge (Review 17)

adapt: to change over time and generations of a species in order to survive in an environment (Review 10)

adaptation: the ability of an organism to survive and reproduce in its environment because of certain special characteristics (Review 9)

air pressure: the force of air molecules pressing on a surface (Review 21)

anther: the part of the stamen that contains and produces pollen (Review 7)

aquifer: a naturally occurring underground reservoir that collects water (Reviews 15, 20)

arthropod: a phylum of invertebrate animals with multi-jointed, segmented limbs, including insects and spiders; almost 80% of all animal species are arthropods (Review 6)

asexual reproduction: reproduction in which the offspring has only one parent; organisms that can reproduce in this way include algae and strawberry plants (Review 8)

atom: smallest particle of an element; the building blocks of matter (Reviews 11, 12)

biodiversity: the variety and balance of species in an ecological community (Review 10)

biome: a large geographic area of the Earth having its own characteristic climate and vegetation (Review 10)

biotic: of or relating to living things (Review 10)

catastrophic disturbance: an unexpected natural event, such as a volcanic eruption, that causes major changes in the surrounding ecosystems (Review 10)

cell: the basic unit of all living things (Review 5)

chemical change: a reaction between substances that results in new substances with different chemical properties being formed (Review 12)

chemical energy: energy contained in the molecular bonds of substances (Review 13)

chemical formula: an expression that shows the composition of a compound by using the symbols for the elements (Review 12)

chemical properties: the characteristics of a substance that describe what will happen when it interacts with other substances (Review 12)

chemical reaction: the process in which the physical and chemical properties of substances are changed into different substances that have their own physical and chemical properties (Review 12)

chemical weathering: the effect of chemicals, such as acid rain, on surfaces, such as rock (Review 19)

chromosome: a threadlike, DNA-carrying strand that makes up the genes that tell what traits an organism will have; chromosomes exist in pairs in all cells except gametes (Review 8)

circuit: a system of electrical parts that provides a path for an electrical current (Review 14)

circulatory system: the body system that uses blood to carry food, water, and oxygen to parts of the body (Review 6)

class: level of classification of living things below phylum and above order; humans belong to class Mammalia (Review 6)

coevolution: evolution involving changes in two or more interdependent species (Review 9)

compound: a chemical substance that is made up of two or more different kinds of atoms that are bonded together (Review 12)

conclusion: a decision based on investigation and evidence (Reviews 1, 2)

condensation: when a gas cools and changes from gas to liquid form (Review 20)

conductor: a material that transmits heat or electricity easily (Review 14)

conservation of energy: the physical law that states that energy cannot be created or destroyed; although it goes through transformations, the total amount of energy always stays the same (Review 13)

critical thinking: clarifying issues, weighing alternatives, making fair and informed judgments, and justifying decisions (Review 3)

data: information that describes events or things, such as temperatures or life spans (Review 2)

degree of confidence: a measurement in formal numbers (for example, probability) or informal words of how strongly a belief is held, given the evidence (Review 3)

density: the amount of mass in a given volume; $density = \frac{mass}{volume}$ (Review 11)

© 2001 Buckle Down Publishing Company. DO NOT DUPLICATE.

dependent variable: the factor in an experiment that changes as a result of a controlled variable (Review 1)

design: a general process for solving technology problems—includes identifying the problem; brainstorming solutions; choosing, implementing, and evaluating a solution; possibly redesigning the solution; and communicating throughout (Review 4)

differential heating effect: the way that regional temperatures on Earth vary as a result of Earth's tilt on its axis and the various amounts of energy it takes to heat different surfaces (Review 21)

digestive system: the group of organs that breaks down food in the body (Review 6)

DNA: deoxyribonucleic acid, the chemical that makes up organisms' genes on each chromosome (Review 8)

dominant trait: the trait that appears in an offspring when two different genes are mixed (Review 8)

dormancy: a state of temporary inactivity into which certain plants and animals go in order to conserve energy in the colder months until the warmer weather returns (Review 10)

dynamic equilibrium: the state that exists when all living and nonliving things on the planet interact in ways that create a living balance (Review 10)

echo: a reflected sound wave that can be heard after a delay (Review 17)

ecology: the study of natural environment systems (Review 10)

ecosystem: all of the living and nonliving things in a given area existing and interacting together (Review 10)

egg: the female sex cell (Review 7)

electric current: the flow of electrons (Review 14)

electrical energy: the flow of electrons among atoms in an object that conducts electricity (Review 13)

electromagnet: a magnet made by running electric current through a wire wrapped around a metal object (Review 14)

electron: a negatively charged subatomic particle that moves in an orbit shell outside of an atom's nucleus (Review 12)

element: a substance that cannot be broken down by simple chemical and physical processes (Reviews 11, 12)

embryo: the early stages of growth after fertilization (Review 8)

endocrine system: the body system that controls body functions with chemicals called hormones (Review 6)

endothermic: a type of chemical change in which energy is absorbed by a substance (Review 12)

energy: the ability to push or pull to do work; examples of different types include electrical, chemical, kinetic, wind, water, and solar (Review 13)

erosion: the breaking down and moving of earth material from one place to another (Review 18, 19)

evaporation: the change of a liquid to a gas (Review 20)

evolution: the adaptation of a species over time to its surrounding environment (Review 9)

excretory system: the group of organs that removes liquid and solid wastes from the body (Review 6)

exosphere: the outer layer of the Earth's atmosphere, beginning at 700 km above the Earth's surface (Review 21)

exothermic: a type of chemical change in which energy is given off (Review 12)

fair test: an experiment in which one independent variable is tested by keeping all other independent variables the same (Review 1)

family: level of classification of living things below order and above genus; humans belong to family Hominidae (Review 6)

fertilization: the process in which the egg and sperm cells of the parent organisms unite in the first stage of sexual reproduction (Reviews 7, 8)

filament: the stalk that bears the anther of a stamen (Review 7)

food chain: the link from a lower organism (a plant, for example) to a higher organism (a rabbit) to a higher organism (a fox), and so on; it is a straight line from bottom to top (Review 10)

force: a push or pull that causes something to change its speed or direction (Review 16)

friction: a force that occurs when two things move past each other and rub together (Review 16)

fulcrum: the point or support around which a lever rotates (Review 16)

gamete: a specialized cell of sexual reproduction; the sperm or egg (Review 8)

© 2001 Buckle Down Publishing Company. DO NOT DUPLICATE.

gene: a unit found on a cell's chromosomes that carries information about a trait of the organism (Review 8)

genetic variability: the range of differences within inherited traits of a species (Review 7)

genetics: the study of how traits are inherited (Review 8)

genus: level of classification of living things below family and above species; humans belong to the genus *Homo* (Review 6)

global warming: the rise in global temperatures; although there is some debate, most scientists believe that it is caused by an increase in greenhouse gases from human pollution (Review 2)

graduated cylinder: an instrument used for the measurement of volume, especially of liquids and irregularly shaped solids (Review 11)

gravity: a force that acts without physical contact to pull two objects toward each other (Review 16)

greenhouse effect: the warming of the Earth as a result of gases in the atmosphere that capture some of the Sun's heat reflected back from the Earth (Reviews 2, 15)

groundwater: water located below ground that constitutes about 0.7% of Earth's water supply (Reviews 15, 20)

heredity: the passing of traits from one generation to the next (Reviews 8, 9)

humidity: the amount of water vapor in the air (Review 20)

hydrocarbon: a compound containing only hydrogen and carbon atoms that occurs naturally in petroleum (Review 15)

hypothesis: an idea, theory, or assumption that can be tested in a scientific investigation (Reviews 1, 2)

igneous rock: rock formed by the cooling of magma or lava (Review 18)

independent variable: a variable that is isolated for study in an experiment (Review 1)

inertia: the tendency of objects to keep doing what they are doing (moving or staying at rest; Review 16)

inference: a conclusion based on limited factual information (Review 2)

invertebrate: an animal that does not have a backbone (Review 6)

ionosphere: the section of the Earth's atmosphere consisting of the mesosphere and part of the thermosphere (Review 21)

irrigation: the practice of diverting water to crops and other human uses (Review 19)

kinetic energy: the energy of moving atoms, particles, or objects (Review 13)

kingdom: highest level of classification of living things; humans belong to kingdom Animalia (Review 6)

lens: the portion of the eye that focuses an incoming wave of light and projects it onto the retina (Review 17)

lever: a rigid body that rotates around a fulcrum; a simple machine (Review 16)

longitudinal wave: waves in which the particles move back and forth in the same direction as the wave's motion; for example, sound waves and seismic (earthquake) waves (Review 17)

magma: hot, molten (liquid) rock material beneath the surface of the Earth (Review 18)

mass: the amount of matter in something (Review 11)

matter: a general term for the material of which all substances are made; anything that has mass and occupies volume (Review 11)

mechanical energy: energy that can move objects (Review 13)

medium: the substance through which a wave travels (Review 17)

meiosis: the process of cell division at the beginning of sexual reproduction that produces gametes with half as many chromosomes as the original cells (Review 8)

mesosphere: the third layer of the Earth's atmosphere, which stretches from about 50 km to 88 km above the Earth's surface (Review 21)

metamorphic rock: igneous or sedimentary rock changed by pressure or heat (Review 18)

meteorologist: a scientist who studies weather (Review 21)

mineral: the pure, crystalline form of nonliving chemical compounds, usually found underground; for example, diamond, sulfur, and salt (Review 18)

mitochondria: organelles that release energy to the rest of the cell (Review 5)

mitosis: the process of one complete cell dividing into two complete cells (Reviews 5, 8)

© 2001 Buckle Down Publishing Company. DO NOT DUPLICATE.

model: a simplified representation of objects, structures, or systems used in analysis, explanation, interpretation, or design (Reviews 2, 4)

molecule: smallest part of a substance that is made up of two or more atoms (Review 12)

multicellular: having more than one cell; humans have trillions of cells (Review 5)

natural selection: survival of the fittest; the organisms that have adapted the best are the ones that will survive and reproduce (Review 9)

nervous system: the body system that controls the flow of information in the body; it is made up of the brain, spinal cord, sensory nerves, and motor nerves (Review 6)

neutron: a particle within an atom's nucleus that has no charge (Review 12)

Newton's first law: if the forces acting on an object are balanced (equal and opposite), the object will continue doing what it is doing; inertia (Review 16)

normal force: the force that pushes up to support the weight of an object (Review 16)

nuclear energy: energy that comes from the nucleus of an atom when it splits apart or joins together with other nuclei (Review 13)

nucleus: the control center of a cell that contains the chromosomes (Review 8)

octet rule: in order to become more stable, atoms will take electrons, lose electrons, or share electrons so that their outermost shell is filled with eight electrons (Review 12)

opaque: not allowing any light to pass through (Review 17)

optic nerve: the nerve that connects the retina to the brain, transmitting visual information (Review 17)

orbit: the path of an object in space as it travels around another object (Review 22)

order: level of classification of living things below class and above family; humans belong to the order Primates (Review 6)

ore: mineral that is mined and refined to obtain valuable materials such as metal (Review 19)

organ: a group of tissues that work together to do a job in the body (Reviews 5, 6)

organ system: groups of organs that work together to perfom a set of functions (Review 6)

organelle: a specialized structure within a cell, such as a mitochondrion or ribosome (Review 5)

outer shell: the outermost layer of electrons in an atom; what combines or reacts in chemical reactions (Review 12)

ovary: the part of the pistil that bears the ovule(s) (Review 7)

ovule: an egg located inside the ovary of a flower (Review 7)

paleontologist: a scientist who explores the fossil record to learn about prehistoric life forms (Review 9, 18)

parallel circuit: a type of circuit in which there is more than one path for the current to travel (Review 14)

periodic table of the elements: a visual representation of all elements arranged in increasing atomic number and grouped according to similar properties (Review 12)

petal: the colorful part of a flower that surrounds and protects the flower's reproductive organs (Review 7)

phase: any of the four states of matter, including solid, liquid, gas, and plasma (Review 11); the different shapes of the Moon as it progresses through a one-month cycle, as seen from Earth (Review 22)

photosynthesis: the process by which plants make food in their chloroplasts from sunlight, water, and carbon dioxide (Review 7)

phototropism: the tendency of plants to bend or lean toward light in order to get the most energy for photosynthesis (Review 10)

phylum: level of classification of living things below kingdom and above class; humans belong to the phylum Chordata (Review 6)

physical change: change in physical properties of a substance without changing the substance itself (Review 11)

physical properties: characteristics of a substance that can be observed without changing the substance in some way, such as its color, hardness, odor, mass, weight, volume, density, and so on (Review 12)

physical weathering: changes on the earth's surface caused by exposure to temperature changes, glaciers, running water, growing roots, and certain human activities (Review 19)

pistil: the female reproductive organ of a flower, consisting of the style, stigma, and ovary (Review 7)

© 2001 Buckle Down Publishing Company. DO NOT DUPLICATE.

pollination: the process of transferring pollen from the stamens to the stigma of a flower (Review 7)

pollution: the introduction of human waste products into the evironment; air, water, land, thermal, and light pollution are major examples (Review 15)

potential energy: energy that is a result of an object's position (Review 13)

precipitation: water that falls to the Earth in various forms, such as rain, snow, or hail (Review 20)

probability: the chance of an event happening determined by dividing the number of desired or undesired events by the total number of possible events (Review 3)

property: a specific feature of something (Review 11)

proton: a positively charged particle in an atom's nucleus (Review 12)

pupil: the hole in the center of the eye through which light passes (Review 17)

radiant energy: energy that can flow through empty space, such as sunlight, radio waves, and X rays (Review 13)

recessive trait: the trait that does not appear in an offspring when two different genes are mixed (Review 8)

reclamation: the process of restoring ecosystems after a technological disruption such as mining; reclamation is never 100% successful (Review 19)

reflection: a wave bouncing off a surface (Review 17)

refraction: light changing direction as it passes from one medium to another, such as between air and water or air and glass (Review 17)

reproduction: the process of producing new organisms in a population (Review 8)

resistance: the measure of the amount of work needed for electrical current to move through a wire or device (Review 14)

respiration: the chemical process by which an organism gets its energy from food (Review 7)

respiratory system: the body system that brings oxygen into the body and eliminates carbon dioxide waste (Review 6)

retina: the membrane lining the interior of the eye; it receives the visual information from the lens (Review 17)

revolve: to travel in a curved path, or orbit (Review 22)

rock: solid mineral material, usually a combination of more than one mineral (Review 18)

rotate: to spin on an axis (Review 22)

runoff: water that is neither absorbed into the Earth nor evaporated into the air and instead runs over the land to waterways (Review 20)

scatter: the process of a wave reflecting in an irregular pattern (in many directions) from an irregular surface (Review 17)

science: inquiry that searches out, describes, and explains patterns in the natural world (Review 4)

sediment: eroded Earth materials that have been deposited by water (Review 18)

sedimentary rock: rock that has been formed from sediment (Review 18)

sepal: one of the outermost petals of a flower that protect the bud (Review 7)

series circuit: a type of circuit in which the current can travel only along a single path (Review 14)

sexual reproduction: the creation of offspring by two parents (Reviews 7, 8)

simple machine: any device that changes forces or direction of forces (Review 16)

skeletal system: the body system made up of the bones that support the body, protect internal organs, and allow the body to move (Review 6)

smog: a dense form of air pollution that results from the reaction of sunlight with automobile exhaust (Review 15)

society: a community or nation of people having many common values, beliefs, traditions, interests, and institutions (Review 4)

solar energy: a source of energy gained by collecting sunlight in special panels (Review 13)

solar system: a system of bodies in space that revolve around a star (Review 22)

sound energy: the longitudinal waves that cause hearing and can travel through a variety of media (Review 13)

species: the smallest and most specific level of classification of living things; humans belong to species *sapiens* (Review 6)

© 2001 Buckle Down Publishing Company. DO NOT DUPLICATE.

sperm: the male sex cell (Review 7)

stamen: the male reproductive organ of a flower, consisting of the anther and filament (Review 7)

stigma: the sticky part of the pistil that traps pollen grains (Review 7)

stratosphere: the second layer of the Earth's atmosphere, which is located from 11 km to 48 km above the Earth's surface (Review 21)

style: the tubelike structure that leads from a flower's stigma to its ovaries (Review 7)

succession: the gradual change in an ecosystem over time (Review 10)

surface mining: a mining process in which the top layer of plants, soil, and rock are completely removed to extract a mineral; also called *strip mining* (Review 19)

system: a method of organizing different parts by looking at how they work together to achieve a specific function (Reviews 2, 4); a group of organs or parts working together to achieve a purpose (Review 5)

systematic investigation: an investigation in which all variables are identified and recorded so that the investigation can be repeated (Review 1)

technology: the application of knowledge to solve problems and make useful things (Review 4)

temperature: the measurement of how fast the particles of matter in an object are moving (Review 11)

thermal energy: the heat energy of all the moving particles in an object (Review 13)

thermal pollution: the release of water that has been heated by human use in home and industry into an ecosystem (Review 15)

thermosphere: the fourth layer of the Earth's atmosphere, extending from 88 km to 700 km above the Earth's surface (Review 21)

tissue: a team of plant or animal cells that does a specific job (Review 5)

topographical map: a map that shows elevation changes and other natural features; also called *contour map* (Review 18)

trait: a characteristic of a living being, such as hair color or eye color (Review 8)

translucent: allowing light to pass through only partially (Review 17)

transparent: allowing light to pass through completely (Review 17)

transverse wave: waves in which the particles move up and down at a right angle to the direction in which the wave travels; for example, light waves and water waves (Review 17)

troposphere: the first layer of the Earth's atmosphere, which stretches from the Earth's surface to an altitude of 11 km; contains all weather (Review 21)

turbine: an engine wrapped with copper wire that is rotated in a magnetic field to make the electrons in the wire move (Review 14)

unicellular: having only one cell (Review 5)

universe: made up of all galaxies and the space in between (Review 22)

vacuum: space that is completely empty of any solid, liquid, or gas (Review 17)

variable: a factor that changes in an experiment (Review 1)

variation: differences between the traits of parents and offspring (Review 8)

vertebrate: an animal with a backbone or spinal cord (Review 6)

vibrations: the back-and-forth motion of an object, medium, or wave (Review 17)

volume: the amount of space an object takes up (Review 11)

water cycle: the process by which water is evaporated from the surface of the Earth by the Sun's energy and later cooled and condensed into precipitation to recycle the water and begin the cycle again (Reviews 20, 21)

watershed: an area of land and bodies of water that drain into a larger body of water (Review 15)

wave: repeating vibrations that travel through space and time (Review 17)

weathering: the wearing down of rocks and soil by chemical and physical processes (Review 18)

work: the amount of force needed to move something a certain distance (Review 13)

zygote: the cell formed when a sperm and an egg combine (Review 8)

© 2001 Buckle Down Publishing Company. DO NOT DUPLICATE.

Michigan Science Content Standards and Benchmarks — Middle School

Sharpen Up on Michigan Science, Book 8, is based on the following Science Content Standards and Benchmarks from the Michigan Curriculum Framework. The workbook has been designed to provide review of the skills and content tested by the Michigan Educational Assessment Program (MEAP). The following table matches the Standards and Benchmarks with the *Sharpen Up* review(s) in which they are addressed.

			Sharpen Up Review(s)
I.	**Constructing New Scientific Knowledge**		
CS1(C)		All students will ask questions that help them learn about the world; design and conduct investigations using appropriate methodology and technology; learn from books and other sources of information; communicate their findings using appropriate technology; and reconstruct previously learned knowledge.	
	1.	Generate scientific questions about the world based on observation.	2
	2.	Design and conduct scientific investigations.	1, 2
	3.	Use tools and equipment appropriate to scientific investigations.	1
	4.	Use metric measurement devices to provide consistency in an investigation.	2
	5.	Use sources of information in support of scientific investigations.	1
	6.	Write and follow procedures in the form of step-by-step instructions, formulas, flow diagrams, and sketches.	2
II.	**Reflecting on Scientific Knowledge**		
CS1(R)		All students will analyze claims for their scientific merit and explain how scientists decide what constitutes scientific knowledge; how science is related to other ways of knowing; how science and technology affect our society; and how people of diverse cultures have contributed to and influenced developments in science.	
	1.	Evaluate the strengths and weaknesses of claims, arguments, or data.	3
	2.	Describe limitations in personal knowledge.	3
	3.	Show how common themes of science, mathematics, and technology apply in real-world contexts.	2, 3, 4, 11
	4.	Describe the advantages and risks of new technologies.	4
	5.	Develop an awareness of and sensitivity to the natural world.	4
	6.	Recognize the contributions made in science by cultures and individuals of diverse backgrounds.	1, 4, 22

© 2001 Buckle Down Publishing Company. DO NOT DUPLICATE.

III. Using Life Science Knowledge		*Sharpen Up* Review(s)
CS1(LC)	All students will apply an understanding of cells to the functioning of multicellular organisms, and explain how cells grow, develop and reproduce.	
	1. Demonstrate evidence that all parts of living things are made of cells.	5
	2. Explain why and how selected specialized cells are needed by plants and animals.	5
CS2(LO)	All students will use classification systems to describe groups of living things; compare and contrast differences in the life cycles of living things; investigate and explain how living things obtain and use energy; and analyze how parts of living things are adapted to carry out specific functions.	
	1. Compare and classify organisms into major groups on the basis of their structure.	6
	2. Describe the life cycle of a flowering plant.	7
	3. Describe evidence that plants make and store food.	7
	4. Explain how selected systems and processes work together in animals.	6
CS3(LH)	All students will investigate and explain how characteristics of living things are passed on through generations; explain why organisms within a species are different from one another; and explain how new traits can be established by changing or manipulating genes.	
	1. Describe how the characteristics of living things are passed on through generations.	8
	2. Describe how heredity and environment may influence/determine characteristics of an organism.	8
CS4(LE)	All students will explain how scientists construct and scientifically test theories concerning the origin of life and evolution of species; compare ways that living organisms are adapted (suited) to survive and reproduce in their environments; and analyze how species change through time.	
	1. Describe how scientific theory traces possible evolutionary relationships among present and past life forms.	9
	2. Explain how new traits might become established in a population and how species become extinct.	9

© 2001 Buckle Down Publishing Company. DO NOT DUPLICATE.

		Sharpen Up Review(s)
III.	**Using Life Science Knowledge** *(Continued)*	
CS5(LEC)	All students will explain how parts of an ecosystem are related and how they interact; explain how energy is distributed to living things in an ecosystem; investigate and explain how communities of living things change over a period of time and analyze how humans and the environment interact.	
	1. Describe common patterns of relationships among populations.	10
	2. Describe how organisms acquire energy directly or indirectly from sunlight.	10
	3. Predict the effects of changes in one population in a food web on other populations.	10
	4. Describe the likely succession of a given ecosystem over time.	10
	5. Explain how humans use and benefit from plant and animal materials.	10
	6. Describe ways in which humans alter the environment.	10, 18, 19
IV.	**Using Physical Science Knowledge**	
CS1(PME)	All students will measure and describe the things around us; explain what the world around us is made of; and explain how electricity and magnetism interact with matter.	
	1. Describe and compare objects in terms of mass, volume, and density.	11
	2. Explain when length, mass, weight, density, area, volume, or temperature are appropriate to describe the properties of an object or substance.	11
	3. Classify substances as elements, compounds, or mixtures, and justify classifications in terms of atoms and molecules.	12
	4. Describe the arrangement and motion of molecules in solids, liquids, and gases.	12
	5. Construct simple circuits and explain how they work in terms of the flow of current.	14
	6. Investigate electrical devices and explain how they work, using instructions and appropriate safety precautions.	1, 14

© 2001 Buckle Down Publishing Company. DO NOT DUPLICATE.

Appendix

IV. **Using Physical Science Knowledge** *(Continued)*	*Sharpen Up* Review(s)
CS2(PCM) All students will investigate, describe and analyze ways in which matter changes; describe how living things and human technology change matter and transform energy; explain how visible changes in matter are related to atoms and molecules; and how changes in matter are related to changes in energy.	
1. Describe common physical changes in matter: evaporation, condensation, sublimation, thermal expansion, and contraction.	12
2. Describe common chemical changes in terms of properties of reactants and products.	12
3. Explain physical changes in terms of the arrangement and motion of atoms and molecules.	12
4. Describe common energy transformations in everyday situations.	13
CS3(PMO) All students will describe how things around us move and explain why things move as they do; demonstrate and explain how we control the motions of objects; and relate motion to energy and energy conversions.	
1. Qualitatively describe and compare motions in two dimensions.	15
2. Relate motion of objects to unbalanced forces in two dimensions.	15
3. Describe the non-contact forces exerted by magnets, electrically charged objects, and gravity.	14, 15
4. Use electric currents to create magnetic fields, and explain applications of this principle.	14
5. Design strategies for moving objects by application of forces, including the use of simple machines.	15
CS4(PWV) All students will describe sounds and sound waves; explain shadows, color, and other light phenomena; measure and describe vibrations and waves; and explain how waves and vibrations transfer energy.	
1. Explain how sound travels through different media.	16
2. Explain how echoes occur and how they are used.	16
3. Explain how light is required to see objects.	16
4. Describe ways in which light interacts with matter.	16
5. Describe the motion of vibrating objects.	15
6. Explain how mechanical waves transfer energy.	16

202

© 2001 Buckle Down Publishing Company. DO NOT DUPLICATE.

V. Using Earth Science Knowledge		Sharpen Up Review(s)
CS1(EG)	All students will describe the earth's surface; describe and explain how the earth's features change over time; and analyze effects of technology on the earth's surface and resources.	
	1. Describe and identify surface features using maps.	17
	2. Explain how rocks are formed.	17
	3. Explain how rocks are broken down, how soil is formed and how surface features change.	17
	4. Explain how rocks and fossils are used to understand the age and geological history of the earth.	17
	5. Explain how technology changes the surface of the earth.	19
CS2(EH)	All students will demonstrate where water is found on earth; describe the characteristics of water and how water moves; and analyze the interaction of human activities with the hydrosphere.	
	1. Use maps of the earth to locate water in its various forms and describe conditions under which they exist.	20
	2. Describe how surface water in Michigan reaches the ocean and returns.	20
	3. Explain how water exists below the earth's surface and how it is replenished.	20
	4. Describe the origins of pollution in the hydrosphere.	18
CS3(EAW)	All students will investigate and describe what makes up weather and how it changes from day to day, from season to season and over long periods of time; explain what causes different kinds of weather; and analyze the relationships between human activities and the atmosphere.	
	1. Explain patterns of changing weather and how they are measured.	21
	2. Describe the composition and characteristics of the atmosphere.	21
	3. Explain the behavior of water in the atmosphere.	21
	4. Describe health effects of polluted air.	18
CS4(ES)	All students will compare and contrast our planet and sun to other planets and star systems; describe and explain how objects in the solar system move; explain scientific theories as to the origin of the solar system; and explain how we learn about the universe.	
	1. Compare the earth to other planets and moons in terms of supporting life.	22
	2. Describe, compare, and explain the motions of solar system objects.	22
	3. Describe and explain common observations of the night skies.	22

© 2001 Buckle Down Publishing Company. DO NOT DUPLICATE.